Forest Bathing

A Nature Book for Adults Looking To Find Good Mental Health

Joanne Hedger

Elemental

Elemental Retail Ltd

© Copyright 2025 - All rights reserved

Legal Notice:

This book is copyright protected. This book is only for personal use. You cannot amend, distribute, sell, use, quote or paraphrase any part of the content within this book, without the consent of the author and publisher.

www.elementalretail.com

Disclaimer Notice:

Please note the information contained within this document is for educational and entertainment purposes only. All effort has been executed to present accurate, up to date, and reliable, complete information. No warranties of any kind are declared or implied. Readers acknowledge that the author is not engaging in the rendering of legal, financial, medical, psychological, or professional advice.

Under no circumstances will any blame or legal responsibility be held against the publisher, or author, for any damages, reparation, or monetary loss due to the information contained within this book; either directly or indirectly.

Contents

Dedication	V
1. Introduction	1
2. Understanding Shinrin Yoku	5
3. Finding Your Place Among the Trees	13
4. Preparation	18
5. Moving Through the Forest	24
6. Obstacles & Adaptations	37
7. The Concrete Jungle	48
8. Through the Seasons	55
9. Solo vs Shared	71
10. After Dark	76
11. Yoga & Meditation	81
12. Eco-Consciousness	87
13. Branching Out	92
14. Cultural Insights	96

15.	Community	106
16.	Bringing Nature Indoors	118
17.	Nature Journaling	123
18.	Daily Routines	127
19.	The Future of Forest Bathing	130
20.	Conclusion	135
	About the author	138
	Your Chance to Help Others...	140
	Books by the Same Author	141
	References	145

To Rais Wood, and all the quiet places that held me when I couldn't hold myself.

Chapter One

Introduction

The argument started over something small, what it was doesn't even matter now. What does matter is the way it left you: heart thumping, chest tight, that hum of frustration ringing loudly in your mind. Grabbing your coat, you stormed out the door, the slam behind you more satisfying than it should've been. The pavement gave way to a path, and before long, you found yourself in the woods.

The air changed. Cooler, calmer, as if the trees themselves were trying to soothe your frustrations. Underfoot, the soft and silent earth absorbed each step, above sunlight danced through the branches, painting patterns on the ground that moved with the breeze. You didn't plan for this, didn't even realize you needed it, but the woods wrapped themselves around you like a hug from a cherished friend. The calm that washed over you wasn't a coincidence. It was something deeper, something ancient. The Japanese call it *Shinrin Yoku*. Forest bathing.

Now, before you start picturing bubble baths surrounded by ferns, forest bathing doesn't involve soap or water. It's about stepping into the forest and soaking up its atmosphere; the sights, sounds, and smells, and not just because it's beautiful (though it is), but because it does something remarkable to you, both physically and mentally. And you don't need a mystical, ancient forest to feel it. Even the scruffy park down the road, with the one wonky bench and the dog-poo bins every 100 yards, has its own quiet magic if you give it a chance.

Let me take you back to my first *real* forest bathing experience. Now, I'm not just some casual tree lover, I'm a full-on tree nut. Whatever the season, the weather, the state of the tree, its location, it doesn't matter, all trees fascinate me, some just take my breath away. The more I learn about them, the more they impress me. They are simply incredible living beings that outlive most of us. As a Druid and proud guardian of a small patch of English woodland, I thought I had trees pretty much sussed. I've hugged them, climbed them, even argued with them no occasion. But this time? This was different. It wasn't just another walk in the woods.

I had not long returned from a year living in the wilds of Africa, training to become a field guide. And let me tell you, that training involved paying attention to *everything*. Listening, looking, touching, and on the occasional weird day... tasting. But after such a prolonged and "off-grid" period, I came back to a shed load of things to get sorted, plans to be made, chores to be seen to. Very quickly that familiar sense of impending overwhelm appeared on the horizon.

So, armed with my newly-acquired awareness skills, and knowing full well that I needed time out surrounded by nature, I decided to head out to my local woods.

I donned the wellies and set off out the back gate on the same one-mile circular walk I've done a thousand times, (which typically takes me 20-30 minutes). Except this time I wasn't walking to cover ground or tick the "I've-been-out-the-house-today" box. I was walking to intentionally observe. To "bathe" in the trees themselves and everything they offer.

After a few minutes walking down past the alotments and across the meadow, I reached the edge of the woods. I stood still, closed my eyes, and waited for the forest to come to me. At first, it felt... awkward. My mind was still buzzing with unanswered emails, finance plans and the mundane, "did I take the chicken out the freezer?" And yet, as I listened intently, surrounded by familiar trees, something started to shift. The forest began to share its magical healing. The tension in my shoulders started to slip away. The chatter in my head began to quiet. Somewhere between the drilling woodpecker and the distant squawks of a magpie, the energy of the forest worked its way into me. It was like hearing a whisper I didn't know I was waiting for: *"Welcome home."*

The forest invited me in and I wandered, I stopped, I wandered some more, I marvelled, I listened and I noticed. That one mile took me almost three hours but I arrived home bursting with energy and enthusiasm. I felt ridiculously alive. The brain fog had cleared and I had fresh ideas to a whole host of issues I had been procrastinating over.

I want you to feel that energy too. I want you to hear that whispered invitation. I want you to be healed and inspired by the trees around you.

This book is me encouraging you to get started, by providing some background information, some tips and tricks and possibly some information that seems really pretty obvious too – but I don't want to assume you know anything about the great outdoors – for all I know, you live in a high-rise block with only a window box and a city view as your starting point, and that's absolutely fine. The good thing about plants and trees is they get everywhere and usually need only sunlight and water to take hold.

Now, you might be thinking, "Do I really need a book to tell me how to go for a walk in the woods?" This book isn't just about putting one foot in front of the other. It's about how to truly slow down, how to notice the quiet wonders you've likely walked past a hundred times. It's about transforming a simple walk into something truly nourishing, helping you get the absolute most from your time amongst the trees.

So, let's step into the forest together. The trees are waiting, and trust me, they've been dying to get a word in.

CHAPTER TWO

Understanding Shinrin Yoku

The air in Tokyo is sharp this morning, the kind of autumn crispness that makes you pull your coat a little tighter. The city hums as it always does. Heels striking pavement, trains rushing past, and screens flashing lives lived at high speed. But if you know where to look, you'll notice something different. A small group of office workers steps away from their desks. No phones, no laptops, no excuses about urgent emails. They just leave.

They drift into a nearby park, moving toward the trees. The leaves above them are on the turn, dropping in slow motion to the ground, as if to remind anyone watching that even here, in the heart of the world's most relentless city, nature still moves at its own pace. They aren't out for a jog or a power walk. They're here for something quieter, more deliberate.

This is **Shinrin Yoku (Forest Bathing)**. It might sound old-fashioned, out of place in a city known for its neon and noise, but its simplicity is its power. In an age where everyone seems to be running toward something, these people have chosen to stop. And in that stillness, under the trees, they're finding something modern life rarely offers: a moment to reconnect, not just with nature, but with themselves.

The Origins of Shinrin Yoku

It might sound like just another wellness buzzword, but hear me out. Forest bathing was born out of necessity. Imagine Japan in the 1980s: technology was booming, cities were buzzing, and people were starting to unravel. Stress levels skyrocketed, screen time crept in, and a gnawing sense of disconnection took hold.

The solution didn't come from a lab or a boardroom; it came from the forests. The Japanese government, recognizing the strain on its people, looked to the country's most abundant resource: its trees. Shinrin Yoku was introduced as a lifeline; a way for people to reconnect with the natural world and, in doing so, reconnect with themselves.

In Japan, nature is sacred. So much more than just a backdrop for weekend picnics or carefully composed Instagram shots. Shinto beliefs teach that *kami* (spirits) inhabit everything from towering trees to flowing rivers. Nature is alive, breathing, and profoundly intertwined with daily life. To the Japanese, when you step into a forest for Shinrin Yoku, you're entering a sacred space.

What's truly remarkable is how this practice has now crossed borders. Whether you're wandering beneath California's ancient redwoods or pausing under an oak tree in the British countryside, Shinrin Yoku taps into something universal. It's a pull we all feel, a need to escape the noise, slow down, and find peace in the natural world.

The impact has been profound. Not only has Shinrin Yoku become a go-to remedy for frazzled minds, but it's also ignited a movement to protect and preserve the very forests that provide this healing. It's a simple yet radical idea: our health is inseparably tied to the health of the planet.

Business owners pay attention... imagine your team of office workers, stressed and scatterbrained, stepping into a park for their daily dose of Shinrin Yoku. At first, their thoughts race with deadlines, meetings, pings. But as they walk together amongst the trees, their stress levels drop, their breathing slows, and the day ahead seems less daunting. They return to their desks with a clarity that no app, Fitbit, or coffee break could ever deliver. Productivity increases, the office atmosphere relaxes and new ideas, thoughts and creativity bubble up throughout the workforce.

That's the beauty of Shinrin Yoku. It doesn't just recharge your batteries; it reawakens something in you. It's a call to return to the earth, to step out of the chaos and into a space where you can simply be. And in that stillness, you'll find something transformative in yourself.

The Forest's Airborne Gifts

In the heart of a forest, a quiet exchange is always happening, a kind of conversation that often goes unnoticed. Yet, its impact can profoundly transform how we feel, both physically and mentally. The trees, in their silent wisdom, release something remarkable into the air: **phytoncides**. These organic compounds are responsible for the familiar smells of pine or earth after rain, but they are also a hidden gift that science is only just beginning to understand.

These compounds are actually the trees' defence mechanism, helping them ward off pests and disease. Acacia trees in Africa, for example, have a clever response when giraffes start munching on their leaves. When sensing damage, the trees release chemicals into the air – specifically ethylene gas – signalling distress. Incredibly, this causes nearby acacia trees to change the taste of their own leaves, flooding them with bitter tannins to make them less palatable, forcing the giraffes to move on to tastier targets further away.

And it's not just trees. Even ordinary grass is part of this chemical conversation. When grazers like cows or deer start chewing, the grass releases compounds called **Green Leaf Volatiles (GLVs)**. One of these, *cis-3-hexenal*, gives that unmistakable scent of freshly cut grass. While we associate it with warm weather and lazy afternoons, to the plant, it's more like a scream for help – a distress signal warning nearby plants and attracting helpful insects. It's one of nature's little ironies that we find a plant's panic so comforting. These chemical signals we benefit from weren't evolved for human wellness; they're part of an ancient defence system we've only recently started properly researching.

Equally, when a pine tree senses a threat, say, from insect pests or fungal infections, it releases phytoncides that act as a natural deterrent, creating a protective shield. These chemicals travel through the air, influencing surrounding trees to produce their own phytoncides, strengthening the entire forest's resistance. This interconnected defence system works almost like a warning network, letting the whole forest know danger is near.

For us humans, this defence mechanism comes with unexpected benefits. When we breathe in phytoncides, we not only get that fresh, calming scent but also a boost to our immune system. Studies show these compounds can increase the activity of **Natural Killer (NK) cells**, which play a role in fighting off viruses and tumours. Essentially, by spending time in a pine forest, we're getting a dose of nature's medicine, supporting our own well-being just as it helps the trees ward off infections.

Your Body in the Woods: The Science Bit

Let's go back to that argument that left you shaken and storming off. Did you notice how, as soon as you stepped into the woods, the world seemed to slow? It's as if the forest spoke to your body: "Let go, breathe, relax those shoulders, stop clenching that jaw." This wasn't just your imagination; your body was responding in ways science is now revealing.

1. **Physiological Responses:** Within minutes of entering the woods, your **blood pressure** begins to drop. Your **heart rate**, which speeds up under stress, finds a steadier rhythm, slowing to match the forest's pace. **Cortisol**, the primary stress hormone, starts to dip, too. Studies show that this isn't a temporary fix; regular forest bathing has a lasting impact on how our bodies manage stress.

2. **Mental Health Benefits:** The effects on your mind are just as impressive. Remember how your thoughts seemed to untangle once you were surrounded by trees? For me, **mental clarity** is one of the forest's greatest gifts. Time spent in forests reduces symptoms of anxiety and depression, earning it the nickname "nature's antidepressant." For precious moments, you can leave the world's noise behind, letting your mind return to a calmer, more focused state.

3. **Cognitive fatigue** – that brain fog familiar after hours of digital overload – also begins to lift. The forest gives your overstimulated brain a break, allowing you to think more clearly, with sharper focus and even increased creativity. You emerge with a fresh perspective, ready to face the world again.

4. **Immune System Boost:** And then, there's your **immune system**. The trees, through their release of those very same phytoncides, help boost it massively. Every deep breath you took, every moment spent in the forest, was helping to recharge your body's defences. It's a biological connection that links us to nature in a way that's still being explored, but the evidence is clear: the forest is literally healing us on a cellular level.

It's no surprise, then, that forest bathing is becoming recognized as a therapeutic practice for both physical and mental health. In some places, doctors are even prescribing time in nature as part of treatment plans and I read an article just this morning explaining how the NHS are being trained by Natural England to work outdoors and treat patients with specific "doses" of nature.

Our Built-In Connection: Biophilia

You know that feeling when you can't wait to get out of the building and into the open, or when a walk along the beach suddenly makes everything feel right again? That deep draw to green spaces, the rush of fresh air, or the sound of crashing waves – it's something profoundly wired into us. It's called **biophilia**, and it's in our bones.

At its core, biophilia is the idea that we are innately drawn to nature, almost like we're built for it. The term was coined by biologist E.O. Wilson, who argued that our connection to the natural world isn't something we acquire, but something we've always possessed, deep in our DNA. This essential, hardwired need has kept us grounded, literally and figuratively, for thousands of years.

Let's take a step back, back to when our ancestors roamed the land, the wild land, not the cities or towns of today. They relied on nature for everything: food, shelter, safety. The land was their lifeblood, and the environment quite simply their survival. That's why today, when we're near water, we feel calm. Or why we can't help but breathe a little easier when we're in the open, surrounded by oxygen-giving trees. These responses are echoes of our evolutionary past, little signals left by our ancestors to remind us where we come from.

Our ancestors, wandering the open plains, knew exactly where to find safety: under the shade of trees, with clear views of the land ahead. Now, thousands of years later, we're still drawn to those same kinds of landscapes. A quiet wooded lake, the solid feel of earth beneath our feet. They're a part of us. Nature, in all its forms, is where we're meant to be. The Aboriginals in Australia know it, the Pygmy tribes of the Amazon know it, and the Bushmen of the Kalahari know it... most of the rest of us have sadly forgotten.

Nature's Absence: The "Nature Deficit"

Fast forward to today, and here we are, living in cities where the nearest patch of grass might be a park five blocks away, if we're lucky. The hustle, the noise, the constant stream of screens, it's easy to forget that we're not made for all of this. Our evolutionary drive for nature hasn't disappeared, but it's been buried under the weight of modern life. And, like that itch you can't quite scratch, when our biophilic needs go unmet, we start to feel it. Stress levels climb, anxiety sets in, and we begin to feel more disconnected, even though we're all supposedly more "connected" than ever.

There's a term for this modern disconnection: "**Nature Deficit Disorder.**" While I'm not a fan of labels (they can oversimplify things), the fact that this one even exists speaks volumes. It's not so much a "diagnosis" as a warning – a symptom of the way we've drifted from the natural world we were once so in tune with. We're seeing heightened rates of mental health issues, stress-related illnesses, and an overwhelming sense of isolation and loneliness in the age of digital everything. As our lives become more urbanised and screen-dominant, the call of the wild gets lost and we're increasingly failing to hear it (or worse, hearing it, but ignoring it).

Topping Up the Tank: Finding Nature's Rhythm

So, what do we do about it? It's simply not practical to escape civilisation altogether (though that does sound tempting sometimes), but we *can* find ways to weave nature back into our everyday lives. Carving out moments in the day to satisfy that deep need for green spaces, fresh air, and natural beauty. I firmly believe the answer lies in bringing the forest back into your daily habits, even if it's just bringing a few houseplants into your apartment to start with.

Simply put, our connection to nature is just as essential as food and water – without it, our bodies are running on empty. We don't need a scientific study to tell us that we feel better when we step outside; we can feel it in our bones.

So, say *Yes* to that camping trip, say *Yes* to that windy walk along the hillside. It's what you were made for.

CHAPTER THREE

Finding Your Place Among the Trees

When I first heard about the "sit spot" during my safari guide training in Africa, I thought, *Brilliant! A chance to sneak in some downtime while pretending to hone my observation skills.* Ten minutes a day, sitting quietly in nature, sounded like a breezy little luxury. But let me tell you, those first few sessions were anything but serene.

Day one, I plonked myself down on a termite mound (rookie mistake) and spent the next ten minutes flicking away tiny fungus-feeders. Day two, I chose a patch of flattened grass only to discover mid-sit that it doubled as something's latrine. Charming. But the hardest part? Sitting still. My brain kept spinning with to-do lists, trivia, and random regrets (like that time I humiliated my best friend at school for getting the words wrong to "Heaven is a place on Earth" by Belinda Carlisle). I wasn't observing anything except how excruciatingly slow ten minutes could feel.

But something happened around day five. I'd found a better spot by then, a shady patch under a mopane tree where the ground was forgiving and the wildlife less... intrusive. I sat down, and for the first time, I stopped *trying* to observe. I just... sat. That's when the world seemed to open up. A glossy starling landed nearby, tilting its head trying to work out whether I was a threat or not. A bushbuck flicked an ear in my direction but didn't bolt. And I swear, I could hear the swirling wind weaving through the grass, almost as if it was a creature on a journey rather than just air flowing through the undergrowth in different directions. It was like nature had been talking all along, and I'd finally tuned in.

By the end of my training, that little sit spot had become a daily ritual I genuinely looked forward to. It wasn't just about spotting changes to increase my situational awareness, it was about grounding myself, feeling small in the best way possible, but part of something bigger than my own overstuffed head at the same time.

Believe me though, when I say you don't need to be in the wilds of Africa to give it a go. Your sit spot could be a bench at the park, a patch of garden, or even a corner by a windowsill overlooking a tree. The magic isn't in the location; it's in the stillness.

Finding Your Forest

What kind of place are we looking for? Not too crowded, not too desolate, and definitely not next to a motorway where you'll be serenaded by the dulcet tones of truck engines every two minutes. You don't need to trek to an enchanted woodland or scale a misty mountaintop to feel nature's magic either. The magic is in how you *experience* the space, not in how Instagram-worthy it looks.

When I was hunting for my first UK sit-spot walking distance from home, I went all in. I spent hours wandering through local woods, inspecting moss-covered logs like a suspicious house buyer checking for dodgy plumbing. Too damp. Too exposed. Too many joggers giving me the side-eye. It was frustrating, and if I'm honest, part of it was because I missed Africa and nothing came close to my remote sit-spot out there. I almost gave up.

But then I realised something: this wasn't a house purchase. I didn't need the perfect location. I just needed a place that felt right. Somewhere I could sit, breathe, and not feel like I was constantly interrupted or at the mercy of the nosey village kids and their endless curiosity.

In the end, my first "official" spot was a modest copse of birches near a footpath. Nothing fancy, but when I sat there, something clicked. The view wasn't vast but extended out across two small fields, the ground smelled like damp silage, and the occasional dog walker gave me a friendly nod instead of a raised eyebrow.

For your own forest bathing sanctuary, start simple. Is there a park nearby? A scruffy patch of trees at the edge of a field? Even a single tree in your backyard can work. The key is finding a place where you feel comfortable enough to slow down and quiet your mind. If it's somewhere you wouldn't mind taking a flask of tea and a packet of custard creams, it's probably a good contender.

Once you've found your spot, visit it a few times. See how it feels in different weather or at different times of day. Is it peaceful? Do you like the way the sunlight falls? Can you sit without fidgeting, or at least without being poked by an unexpected thorn? Over time, you'll know when you've found *your* place; a corner of the natural world that feels like it's welcoming you back, every time you visit.

Remember, forest bathing isn't about impressing anyone. It's about finding a space where you can let go, breathe, and reconnect with nature. That's all.

Urban Opportunities

You don't need to venture far to find a touch of nature in the city. Urban parks, with their sprawling lawns and towering trees. Green rooftops, magical hidden gems, are popping up in cities worldwide. Then there's botanical gardens, arboretums and churchyards. If fact, so many possible options I've dedicated the whole of chapter seven to it.

Rural Access

For those with access to rural areas or happy to venture a bit further, the options for finding your spot truly expand.

National parks and nature reserves often boast well-marked trails ranging from easy walks to more challenging hikes. Before you go, a quick online search can provide you with trail maps, difficulty levels, and must-see spots within these natural areas.

Local nature centers and wildlife trusts can also be invaluable resources, offering guided walks that can enrich your forest bathing experience with educational insights into the local ecosystem. They are also often less crowded, providing a more intimate connection with the local flora and fauna.

Safety Considerations

I know this might seem obvious, but this is important, and worth repeating, (even if you are an experienced hiker). If you are venturing into rural areas remember;

1. Always let someone know where you're going and when you expect to return, especially if you're going somewhere remote. A twisted ankle can trash a walk and if no-one is likely to find you for a few hours, it could be a cold and painful wait.

2. Stick to marked tracks or ones you know well to avoid getting lost.

3. Be mindful of the weather, terrain and sunset times. Remembering that you'll meet darkness much earlier under the cover of trees.

4. Dress appropriately for the conditions.

5. Always carry water, a map, and a basic first aid kit (see next chapter).

Remember, your safety is paramount; nature can be as unpredictable as it is beautiful.

Community Resources

The journey to find your forest doesn't have to be a solo endeavor either. Local hiking groups and online communities can be gold mines of information and support. Chapter nine explores this in greater detail.

So find a place, sit yourself down, and let the world reveal itself on its own terms. You might be surprised by what you notice, and even more surprised by what you feel.

To increase your chances of having a successful "bath", let's take a brief look next at preparing yourself both practically and mentally.

Chapter Four

Preparation

What to Bring: Essentials for a Day Among the Trees

If you're planing to make a day of it, a bit of thoughtful packing is worth considering. No need to channel Bear Grylls or overthink it; just a few essentials to keep you comfortable, safe, and tuned into the experience without dragging half your house along.

Dressing the Part

This isn't a catwalk, and no one's grading your fashion choices, but dressing wisely can make or break your day;

- **Layers are lifesavers:** Weather in the woods is unpredictable; it's sunny one minute, chilly the next. A fleece or light jacket is your "just in case."

- **Footwear:** Flip-flops? Not unless you love constantly pausing to remove twigs and bits of grass from your toes. Go for boots or trainers that grip and protect, your ankles will thank you.

- **Bug and bramble armor:** Long sleeves and trousers might not scream glamour, but they'll keep the scratches and bites to a minimum.

What's in the Bag?

Forest bathing is all about simplicity, but let's not go full minimalist monk from the start. A few carefully chosen items can make your outing a breeze:

- **Water:** Non-negotiable. Dehydration isn't fun. A reusable bottle keeps things eco-friendly, but handsfree bladder-bags are a game-changer.

- **Snacks:** Think fuel, not feast. Nuts, fruit, or something that doesn't crinkle like a megaphone in a quiet glade.

- **First-aid kit:** My first aid instructor will scorn me for saying this, but unless you are tour leader responsible for a dozen people, stick to just the basics; a plaster for the odd scrape, your epi-pen if you know you react to insect stings, and maybe some citronella spray if you're sweet enough to attract the attention of flying, biting things. It is a balance, you dont want to be caught short if a serious accident happens of course, but be realistic. People have walked the earth for centuries without carrying a giant bag of unneccesary emergency items "just in case".

- **Bag (and space) for Rubbish;** I really wish I didnt need to suggest this, but even in the remotest of places I have come across deflated helium balloons stuck in bushes, coke cans and sweet wrappers.

The golden rule of forest bathing: Keep it simple. If it doesn't add to your comfort or safety, it's probably just a distraction.

Be a Polite Visitor

You're a guest remember. Treat the forest the way you'd want someone to treat your home.

- **Leave no trace:** The forest doesn't need your granola bar wrappers or even your banana skins. Pack it all back out.

- **Respect the locals:** Admire the squirrels from afar. No touching, no feeding.

- **Stick to the trail:** Wandering off-piste damages habitats, especially ground-nesting birds nests (it also increases your chances of getting lost).

- **Keep the volume down:** Let the forest do the talking. Remember, you've got two ears and just one mouth, life tends to work better when you use them in that ratio.

Mental Preparation

The most important step in forest bathing isn't the one you take onto the path, it's the one you take in your mind before you even get there. Preparing yourself mentally turns a simple woodland walk into something deeper and more meaningful. It's about giving the experience room to unfold while setting yourself up to truly be present.

When I go on a multi-day hike, I like to repeat a few words each morning just before I set off – words that ask mother nature to give me plenty of opportunities to learn, an abundance of flora and fauna to marvel at and fascinating wildlife activity for me to observe. I tell her my eyes and ears are open and my memory is ready to hold everything she can throw at me. I tell her I will leave only footprints and take away only photographs (and any litter I come across). Then I run through a mental checklist of things to "notice", starting with the sky and working downwards, so I might check out the weather in all directions, patterns in the clouds and what direction the wind is coming from. Then I might move down to the eye-level big picture, noticing the position of the sun and the long early morning shadows that it casts across the land ahead. This short observational checklist tunes my mind into my surroundings and helps to bring my focus to the present moment. Then I set off.

Setting Your Own Intention

Are you seeking peace, clarity, inspiration, or maybe just a break from the world? Hold that idea loosely as you walk. You'll find it guides you without controlling you.

- Start with something simple, like "I want to feel calmer" or "I'm here to notice new flowers."

- Pause before entering the forest to take a deep breath and think about finding what you need.

- And if it feels natural, share your intention with the forest; a quiet whisper or even just a thought in your mind.

Intentions are a guide; expectations are a trap. It's easy to enter the forest with a script in your head; "I'll feel peaceful," "I'll spot a deer," "It'll be magical", but nature doesn't work like that. Forest bathing is at its best when you let it surprise you. It might be the sound of one bird mimicking another or the odd-shaped mushroom by your boot that makes the day memorable. Be open to it all.

Emotional Readiness

Just like the ocean, the forest has a way of stirring things up. Its' stillness and simplicity can unearth feelings you didn't realize you were carrying. You might find unexpected joy, a gentle sadness, or a quiet release. Being emotionally ready means giving yourself permission to feel whatever comes up, without judgment.

- Acknowledge that emotions may surface and welcome them. I'll never forget the time I walked into the woods an emotional wreck; tired, hormonal and still sobbing. The day had been a mess; upsetting news, a cancelled catch-up, and a clumsy kitchen incident that had me sweeping an entire sack of rice from every single crack in the floor boards. I wasn't expecting the forest to fix me, but it did something even better: it let me feel.

- If it feels too much to walk, find a spot to sit and breathe. Once, during a lone winter walk, I spotted a blackbird perched, all fluffed up on a frosty branch trying to keep warm, and out of nowhere, tears welled up. It wasn't sadness or joy. It was something I couldn't name but needed to feel (or maybe just something I needed to release?). That's the beauty of being in the forest. It allows those buried feelings to rise, not as intrusions but as gifts. If you find yourself overwhelmed, don't fight it. Sit down. Let the trees absorb some of the weight. Feel the ground beneath you; it's solid, and so are you.

- Bring a journal if writing helps you process. Sometimes the act of putting pen to paper is the first step in letting things go. For me, there's something almost sacred about my small woodland notebook. It's not for writing essays or grocery lists, it's solely for catching fleeting moments. Jotting down a thought, a feeling, or even just a short description of the experience, the weather or recording the date the bluebells bloomed.

There's no right or wrong way to do this. The forest is a safe space. It's not there to fix you or give you answers. It's there to let you be you, fully and unapologetically. Whether you're laughing, crying, or just soaking in the silence, the forest welcomes it all.

So the next time you head out, leave the need for perfection behind. Bring your full self; the happy, the anxious, the confused, and even the slightly grumpy version. The forest can handle it, from your buzzing thoughts to the grit under your wellies. And more often than not, you'll leave feeling a little lighter, a little more yourself, and a lot more connected to the world around you.

CHAPTER FIVE

Moving Through the Forest

Breathing Techniques

We breathe all the time, but how often do we notice it? Really notice it?

Try this simple rhythm: inhale for three steps, exhale for three. It sounds ridiculously straightforward, but as you find the pattern, you'll realize your body and the forest are syncing. Once, mid-walk, I caught myself unconsciously matching my breath to the rise and fall of bird calls. It felt oddly poetic, like I'd slipped into the soundtrack of the woods.

Why? you might ask; what's the point? The important thing to note is that the whole time you are focused on your breathing, you are giving your brain a break from dealing with everything else going on in your daily life. Rest-assured, busy brains in the modern world welcome this break.

Awareness

Field guide training involves spending hours each day walking the bush, observing, testing your senses and learning all about your surroundings, but in doing so, you become part of those surroundings, you notice how loud your footsteps are, how your breathing changes on different terrain and how the wind can one minute be in your face and the next be at your back.

It's a small step for your thoughts to then connect your presence and place within the habitat, to the impact you might be making. Can the moles deep in their tunnels beneath my feet judge my weight by the heaviness of my footfall? Do the butterflies mistake the coloured patterns on my top for real flowers? did me turning over that stone with my size fives take the roof off a beetles home?

Slowing down in the woods is a revelation. Instead of striding ahead, try pausing. Not just once or twice but every few steps. Take a moment to notice what your feet are feeling. The squelch of mud, the softness of moss, the sturdiness of a root beneath your sole. Which tree does that root belong to? What messages are being passed along it right now? When you walk slowly, not only does your body slow, but your thoughts do too.

This isn't about staring wistfully into the distance for hours on end trying to keep the to-do list at bay in your mind. It's about seeing, noticing what's really there.

One afternoon, on a well-worn woodland walk, I stopped to look at an unfamiliar leaf to try and ID the tree. To do this, you can't just glance at it, you have to look, really look. I noted the edges of the leaves were laced with tiny teeth, its veins a roadmap of life-giving precision. I inspected the twig that held the leaf, followed a tiny beetle as it made it's way back along the twig to the branch and then noticed a spider crouching within the branch's rough bark, it's numerous eyes, possibly wide in fear at the sheer size of mine staring back. That one leaf turned into an hour of finding beauty and knowledge I'd otherwise have walked straight past, (and the tree species is no longer unfamiliar to me).

Before we set off on safari in Africa, my guests would often tell me they wanted to see Leopards, and I would say ok, well in that case, our best chance to see Leopard is to go birding. Setting the intention to see something huge and then finding it when you stop for something small is such a common occurrence that it cannot be coincidence. I believe it is because when we stop, slow down and spend some time quietly focusing on the small stuff, not only do we notice much more, but the animals consider us as less of a threat, which means they relax too and go about their business in a natural way rather than taking cover.

Leopards are territorial so they are in their own carefully marked territory somewhere all the time, but only by really looking and listening do we start to pick up the clues to their exact location. Clues that were there all along. The monkeys alarm-calling from the trees, the antelope all looking nervously in one direction, on guard. The vultures sitting in wait for their turn at the Leopard's hidden carcass. Such clues are abundant in nature the world over. We dont have to be on safari in deepest Africa to take advantage of them. That blackbird making all the racket in the oak tree is likely trying to move a predator away from her nest. Go check it out, take your binoculars and you might just find a Tawny owl or a buzzard nearby.

Pause. Look up. The canopy above is like a swirling ocean ceiling.

Look down, where fungi are quietly running their underground empires trading messages, nutrients and life-giving water.

Look around, because the forest's stories are never in one place and one story always leads to another.

Land Snorkelling

There's a new term I love, not scientific, but somehow perfect: *land snorkelling*. It describes that slow, curious way of moving through nature, as if the ground were a coral reef and you were floating above it, peering into tiny worlds. You're not walking with purpose, you're meandering. Following the shape of a mossy log. Noticing a cluster of fungi under a leaf. Pausing to admire the lichen patterns on bark like some kind of ancient map.

I attended a talk during guide training which stuck with me ever since. The speaker was a top-quality female guide with many years experience and an overwhelming bucket of knowledge. She shared her theory on the only three questions a guide needed to answer when coming across something on a nature walk;

1. What is it?

2. What's it doing?

3. What's it going to do next?

In forest bathing, we talk a lot about presence. Land snorkelling *is* presence. It's the opposite of marching, of checking your watch, of reaching the summit. It's how you notice the tiny wren watching you from a bramble arch. How you realise the leaves have started to turn. It's slow magic. And you can do it anywhere there's ground to be curious about.

Gratitude

Gratitude turns what you have into more than enough. It shifts your focus from what's missing to what's present, and in the forest, that's everything. By practicing gratitude, you deepen your bond with the natural world.

- As you walk, take a moment to silently thank the forest for its offerings; a bird's call, the texture of moss, even the earthy smell of the ground.

- When your walk is over, reflect on what moved you. Maybe it's the way the trees shaded you and shared their healing gifts or the unexpected calm in your chest.

- Jot down a few notes of gratitude if you like. I tend to just record a voice note on my mobile phone. Either way, they'll remind you later of what the forest gave you.

Sensory Engagement

Imagine being blindfolded and dropped into a forest. No signs, no maps, no GPS. Would you still know you were in a forest? The answer's probably yes, and that's thanks to your senses. Even without sight, your body would start picking up clues; the smell of damp leaves, the softness of moss underfoot, the way birdsong carries through the trees.

We're taught to think our way through the world. To analyse, label, and explain. But when you step into a woodland, thinking can only take you so far. Forest bathing is a sensory exercise, not an intellectual one. It begins with the body.

Long before language or logic came along, our senses were how we first learned to connect with the world. They still work that way, if we let them. Sight, sound, smell, touch, taste, they bring us back to where we are, not where we think we *should* be. And they remind us that we're animals too. Creatures in a living world, not just observers of it.

So this next part isn't a list of things to tick off. It's just a way of noticing what your body already knows.

Focus on just one sense at a time, let each one do what it does best...

Sight

The first thing you'll notice about the forest is its colours. Let's talk about green for a moment. The colour with the widest range of tones of all the colours in the natural world. In colour psychology, green is associated with balance, renewal, and calm. It's considered a restful colour for the human eye and is known to reduce stress and anxiety. Studies have shown that exposure to the colour green, especially in natural settings, can lower blood pressure, improve mood, and even enhance cognitive functioning. This is part of what makes forest bathing so restorative: the abundance of green also stimulates our parasympathetic nervous system, encouraging relaxation and emotional equilibrium.

Perfectly contrasting with the deep greens of the trees, are the bright bursts of woodland flowers, the play of light through the canopy, and the dance of shadow patterns on the forest floor. But once you stop just looking and actually *see*, you start noticing the smaller, subtler details too. The patterns.

Ferns and bracken leaves in late spring unfurling in a perfect demonstration of the mathematical Fibonacci sequence. Spider webs that criss-cross the cavities of a long-dead fallen tree trunk, smooth bark adorned with silvery slug trails and tiny rodent teeth marks still visible on the shells of last year's hazelnuts.

Then there's the tonal shift as the weather changes. Sunlight sharpens the edges of everything, while mist softens it all into a dreamscape. Look up, and you'll see the patchwork of canopy shapes, each species offering a slightly different filter for the light. Can you trace the outline of each tree species above you? do they overlap? who occupies the top spot?

Look down, and you'll spot lichen in delicate mint-greens and pale blues clinging to dead stormfall logs like messy splodges of paint. Even the mud has layers, dark, glossy streaks where badgers have padded past, scattered with crisp leaf outlines that only appear after a rain shower.

Why not stick a magnifying glass in your pocket and open up a whole other level to your observation. Even slugs and snails can be seen as attractive when viewed through a macro lens.

Sound

Close your eyes for a moment, it's easy to get lost in the noise of our everyday lives, but the forest invites you to listen. Really listen. Try picking out individual sounds; the insects buzzing past your ears, branches squeaking and creaking against each other, the far-off chatter of a woodpecker, or the sound of the earth itself shifting underfoot. Notice how the forest's rhythm changes with every step, every breeze, every movement in the distance.

I like to start with what sounds I can identify really close to me: my breathing, the fabric of my clothes rustling against each other and maybe my feet hitting the woodland floor, then I work my way further out, what can I hear within five metres, ten, fifty? what noises can I distinguish further away, maybe up in the sky or off in the distance? Then I work my way back again until I settle in on the sound of my breathing again.

Sometimes it's birdsong, clear and insistent; robins ticking away like little metronomes, or the melodic fluting of a blackbird just before dusk. Other times it's more ambient than that: the slow creak of a tree shifting in the wind, a dead twig falling somewhere unseen, or the soft *plop* of something (probably the wind) dislodging a clump of wet leaves.

You might hear the quick, dry scuffle of a squirrel darting across bark, or the clumsy wingbeat of a woodpigeon overhead, so much louder than you'd expect for something that size. Rain brings its own soundtrack too: the soft patter of droplets on leaf litter, or the sharper tap of water hitting sturdier holly and ivy leaves.

In summer, there's the background hum of insects; bees investigating bramble flowers, the sharp zip of a fly changing direction mid-air, or the rhythmic stridulation of crickets if you're lucky enough to be near a sun-warmed patch.

And if you're near water, whether it's a stream, a boggy hollow, or even just a puddle, you might catch frogs calling, or the occasional splash as something slips in unseen. Even mud makes noise when you're really listening. That faint, satisfying squelch underfoot. Or that odd, hollow *thwop* sound when you pull your boot free.

The more you listen, the more you hear. And the less the 'noise' from outside the forest seems to matter.

Smell

Some scents hit you as soon as you step into the woods, especially after rain in a bluebell wood. Aside from the breath-taking bluebells themselves, there's that rich, earthy smell of damp soil, leaf litter, and things quietly breaking down. It's called *petrichor*, that scent after rain, and it's one of the forest's oldest perfumes. It happens because during dry weather, plants release oils into the soil and rocks. When it finally rains, those oils mix with a compound made by soil-dwelling bacteria called *geosmin*, and together they create that fresh, comforting scent we often associate with the woodland after rain.

> Geosmin is formed from the Greek words for "earth" and "smell" and is detectable by humans at extremely low concentrations (in fact we are better at detecting Geosmin than sharks are at detecting blood in water!). I wonder why? Why did our ancestors need to be able to detect it so easily? To find water quickly after a dry spell maybe?

But if you pause, and let your nose do what it's built for, there's more...

There's the resinous tang of pine or spruce on a warm day, especially if the sun's been heating the bark. Or the dry, peppery note of bracken in late summer. Some trees have their own signature scent; crushed bay leaves, wild garlic, elderflowers, sweet chestnut, or even the faint marzipan smell of meadowsweet if you're near a stream.

The scent palette shifts with the seasons too; Spring smells green and slightly sharp, like nettles and new growth. Autumn smells like mushrooms and rotting leaves, nothing unpleasant, just that damp, nutty, fungal richness that tells you everything's being recycled.

Get close to things and you'll notice more: the clean, lemony snap of birch twigs, the musty smell of moss, or the sudden hit of fox if one passed by earlier. Even fungi have their own catalogue of smells; some like bread flour, others more like wet wool or even seafood.

And then there's smoke. If someone's had a campfire, you'll smell it before you see it. Woodsmoke drifting low and mingling with the undergrowth. It's amazing how scent can drop you straight into a memory. One breath and you're five years old again, collecting dry sticks for kindling with muddy knees.

When you're present with the forest on a regular basis, scent stops being background. It becomes part of the map, part of how you find your way around.

Touch

We don't often think about touch when we're outdoors, especially if it's below zero and your hands are snug in your pockets, but the forest is full of textures. You don't have to go around hugging all the trees (unless you want to), but slowing down enough to actually notice how things feel can add to your whole experience.

There's the rough, ridged bark of an old oak; solid, grooved like a landscape in miniature. Compare that with the papery flake of silver birch, or the almost velvet feel of young hazel twigs. Run your hand along a moss-covered log and you'll feel the difference: cold, springy, sponge-like. Alive.

Touch the leaf litter underfoot, it's dry and brittle in autumn, spongy and slippery after rain. Pick up a fallen feather, or the smooth spiral of a snail shell. Some things surprise you: the rubbery flesh of a fungus, or the weird softness of deer antler velvet if you're lucky enough to find a shed piece.

I love finding new textural contrasts too. Like seeing a polished smooth conker peeking out from a painfully prickly casing, or noting how some leaves are shiny on the upper surface but hairy underneath.

Even the air has a texture. Cool and damp in hollows, warmer and lighter in sun patches. On a breezy day you can feel the trees moving around you, not just hear them, but actually sense the shift in pressure as branches sway and leaves lift.

If you walk barefoot (carefully), there's a whole new set of sensations: the prick of dry pine needles, the chill of mud, the smoothness of stones warmed by the sun. It's easy to forget how many nerve endings we have in our hands and feet until something wakes them up.

Letting your body notice where it is, how it connects with what's around you, can anchor you faster than any to-do list or mindfulness app ever will.

Taste

Taste is the most intimate of the senses because you're not just observing something, you're letting it in. And when it comes to the forest, that can be a powerful experience... *if you know what you're doing*.

If you're familiar with the safe, edible plants of the woods, tasting the land adds another layer entirely. The sharp tang of a wild blackberry, still warm from the sun. The lemon-zing of wood sorrel nibbled straight from the ground. That oddly satisfying sludge of young nettle leaves (once cooked, of course), or the cooling hairy tingle of fresh mint growing where the ground stays damp.

Stream water, when it's safe, tastes like nothing and everything all at once; mineral-rich, cold, clean. It's a world away from the chlorinated tap stuff we're used to.

But taste in the forest isnt just what can be foraged. If you really pay attention, even the air has flavour. Breathe deep and you can sometimes catch a trace of pine resin, or that mushroomy tang that means something's fruiting nearby. It's subtle, but it's there. Like the difference between smelling rain and tasting it on the wind.

A few easy wild nibbles to get to know

If you're curious about tasting the forest, here are a few options that are generally safe, easy to recognise, and not likely to land you in hospital *as long as you're 100% sure what you're picking!*

- **Young Beech leaves** – Fresh, pale green, and slightly lemony. Best in spring before they toughen.

- **Hawthorn leaves** – Sometimes called "bread and cheese" by old foragers. Mild and nutty in spring.

- **Birch leaves** – Slightly bitter, a bit citrusy. Young leaves only.

- **Wood sorrel** – Heart-shaped leaves with a sharp lemon taste. Easy to spot, but don't overdo it (it contains oxalic acid).

- **Wild garlic (ramsons)** – Broad, glossy leaves that smell like garlic. Found in damp woodlands in spring, often in big patches.

- **Blackberries** – Obvious and delicious in late summer. Avoid ones too close to roadsides or low down on dog-walking paths.

- **Nettles** – Only the top few leaves of young plants. Must be cooked or wilted to neutralise the sting.

- **Cleavers (goosegrass)** – Sticky little herb. Mild and cucumbery when young. Can also be steeped into a refreshing tea.

Just remember: no guessing games. If you're not 100% sure what something is, leave it. Always use a good ID guide, pick away from roads and verges at dog-peeing height, and never eat a plant you're not completely sure of. The forest has plenty to offer without needing to play roulette with your insides.

Full Immersion

When you let your senses lead, the forest becomes beautiful scenery that you're part of. It's not about ticking boxes, *seen a bird, heard a twig snap, touched some moss, done.* It's about showing up fully. With your eyes open, your ears tuned in, your hands curious, your nose awake, and maybe even your taste buds (if you're confident and careful).

We spend so much of our lives in our heads; thinking, planning, scrolling, worrying. But your senses? They only operate in the present. They don't care about your deadlines. They can't remember yesterday or predict next Tuesday. They just *are*. And that's what makes them so powerful when it comes to slowing down and reconnecting.

Forest bathing is about *noticing* more, not *doing* more. And the more you notice, the more you belong, right there in that patch of woodland, with the bluetits, the rotting logs, the breeze in the bracken, and whatever version of yourself showed up that day.

So next time you're out there, try letting your body do the noticing before your brain gets involved.

CHAPTER SIX

Obstacles & Adaptations

We all know the feeling. You've promised yourself you'll spend more time outdoors. The forest is calling, and yet... the list of reasons not to go grows longer than your actual to-do list.

The thing is, often these reasons aren't really about a lack of desire. They're just the clever ways our busy minds find to keep us stuck in old routines. And that doesn't make them any less convincing.

In this chapter, we'll take a look at some of the most common hurdles that pop up when you're trying to make forest bathing a regular part of your life. I'll also share a few simple ways to gently move past them. Because, let's face it, the trickiest part is often just getting started.

Obstacle #1 – "I Don't Have Time"

If we're really honest, most of us manage to squeeze in time for things that don't always serve us best, like a bit of aimless scrolling on our phones or getting lost in another TV series. It's not so much about there not being enough hours in the day, but more about how we choose to spend those precious minutes.

Every single person on the planet has the same 1,440 minutes each day. How we spend them is mostly up to us.

Micro-bathing

Think of it as the espresso shot of forest bathing, a quick, potent dose of nature that fits into any schedule. It's about finding small pockets of green in your day and engaging with them mindfully. Chapter 18 covers this in greater detail but for now, consider these simple ideas;

- **Morning routine**: Instead of checking your phone first thing, try spending those first few minutes with a houseplant or by an open window. Let the fresh air wake you up naturally. For me it's filling the bird feeders in winter or harvesting raspberries in summer to plop straight on top of my cereals.

- **Commute creativity**: If you walk or bike to work, try taking a route that passes through a park or along a tree-lined street. Driving? Park a block or two away from your destination and walk the rest of the way, paying attention to any greenery you pass.

Scheduling Time

Treating forest bathing like any other important appointment on your calendar can be a game-changer. It's about prioritizing this time as you would a dental or doctor's appointment because, in essence, it's an investment in your health and well-being.

- **Weekly planner**: Dedicate a slot each week for a longer forest bathing session. Even just an hour on a Saturday morning can recharge you for the days ahead.

- **Alerts and reminders**: Use your phone or calendar app to set reminders for short nature breaks throughout your day. A five-minute pause to step outside or gaze at a tree can be incredibly refreshing.

- **Colour coding**: I tend to mark any outdoor activities (gardening, foraging, woodland management tasks etc.) on my calendar in green. So that, at a glance, I can see if I have sufficient "green time" planned throughout my week or if I need to make more space/time.

Combining Activities

Why not double up? Combine forest bathing with activities already cemented into your routine. It's about being efficient with your time while enriching your experiences.

- **Walking meetings**: Suggest having meetings or brainstorming sessions outdoors, walking side-by-side. The change of scenery might just spark new ideas.

- **Family time**: Turn family catch-ups into nature explorations. A picnic in the park, a weekend hike, or a visit to a botanical garden can be both fun and restorative.

Quality over Quantity

It's not about how long you spend in nature but how you spend that time. Even brief interactions, when approached mindfully, can build a deeper connection with the natural world. Practice fully immersing yourself in the experience, whether it's for five minutes or fifty. Notice the details, the textures, patterns, colours, and let them fill your senses. Use these moments to reflect on what you're thankful for.

Fitting forest bathing into a hectic schedule might feel like trying to wedge one more thing into an already bursting bag, but it's far more doable than it seems. The trick is to start small, stay consistent, and remind yourself that every little moment with nature adds up over time.

Obstacle #2 – "There's Nowhere to Go"

Sometimes it feels like the concrete jungle has us completely surrounded. Roads stretching endlessly, buildings reaching skyward, and not a single patch of green in sight. But don't be fooled, nature is sneaky and defiant. It has a way of infiltrating even the busiest of cities, showing up in places we might not think to look.

Urban Nature Spots

Pop on your urban explorer hat, because cities aren't all concrete and pipework. They're teeming with life, full of hidden ecosystems that just need a second glance and in the next chapter, we'll dive deeper into how to find and make the most of these urban green havens.

Connecting Remotely

Sometimes the woods feel a world away, and that's okay. Technology can actually lend a hand here. While it might sound a bit counterintuitive for a nature practice, you can bring a little slice of the natural world into your day without even stepping outside.

- **Nature Soundscapes:** Slip on some headphones and let the world around you melt away. From exotic rainforest showers to springtime birdsong, these recordings can transform even the noisiest kitchen into a peaceful glade. You can find these on YouTube or apps dedicated to sound therapy.

- **Virtual Reality (VR) Experiences:** Fancy strolling through a rainforest or wandering across Arctic tundra without leaving your sofa? A VR headset can drop you right into these incredible landscapes. It's not quite the real thing, you won't benefit from the phytoncides of course, but given our proven calming reaction to the colour green, it's a pretty good stand-in when you need a quick reset or are unable to get out. Many VR platforms offer nature walks, and they can be surprisingly immersive.

- **Nature Shows and Documentaries:** Sometimes you just need a nature fix from the comfort of your couch. Shows like *Planet Earth*, *Springwatch*, *The Secret Life of Trees*, or *Our Planet* offer stunning visuals and calming narration. These shows may not replace the real thing, but they can be an emotional reset, offering a brief but powerful escape.

- **Live Feeds from Wildlife Trailcams and Nestcams:** There's something hypnotic about watching a badger family go about their nightly routine or wading birds digging for worms in real-time. Websites like Explore.org offer live feeds of nature around the globe, and many wildlife organisations run cams at known habitats. From watching elephants at a watering hole in the wild to seeing a kingfisher at work, it's like a mini-window into nature, available at any moment.

Creating Nature at Home

Your home doesn't need to be a palace to feel like a sanctuary. Even the smallest space can echo nature's calm if you bring a bit of the outdoors inside. Here are some brief examples, expanded upon on in Chapter 16;

- **Indoor plants**: These leafy companions are essential to me, they clean the air, reduce mold, and brighten my mood. Whether it's a compact succulent or a sprawling ivy, a bit of greenery makes a world of difference.

- **Natural materials:** Wood, stone, bamboo – these elements bring a lovely tactile connection to the outdoors. Whether it's a bamboo placemat, a piece of driftwood used as a picture frame, or a stone candleholder, little touches often make a much bigger impact than we realise.

- **Nature-themed art:** Surround yourself with landscapes that move you. A favourite forest photo, a peaceful seaside painting, or a vase of freshly picked wildflowers can be your everyday window to the natural world.

Reframing Perspectives

If you're still thinking, *But where's the nature?*, it might be time for a gentle shift in your focus. Sometimes, it's simply about learning to see what's already there.

Slow down and zoom in. Look at how moss creeps along a brick wall, how dandelions bravely push through pavement cracks, or how pigeons carve clumsy flight paths through the sky. Nature is quite literally everywhere. It's in the details, the cracks, the corners. It's in your headphones, on your rooftop, in the raindrop drawing a path down your kitchen window and in the dust motes sparkling in the sunlight. By gently shifting your perspective and making small changes, you'll discover that even in the busiest city, the natural world is right there, surrounding you.

Obstacle #3 – "I Feel Silly Doing This"

I completely get it. Feeling self-conscious can be a huge barrier, especially when we're doing something a bit unfamiliar. I remember the first time I tried yoga in a class. There I was, craning my neck to see if I was doing the poses "right," worrying that everyone could tell I had no idea what I was doing. It wasn't exactly the relaxing experience I'd imagined. Forest bathing can feel the same way at first, awkward, unsure, like everyone else knows a secret you've somehow missed. But I've realised something important: nature isn't judging you. There's no "right" or "wrong" way to be in the woods. No one's really watching, and if they are, they're probably more concerned with their own experience anyway.

Starting Small

One of the easiest ways to ease into forest bathing without feeling self-conscious is to start in spaces where you already feel comfortable. A more secluded spot can help take the pressure off and give you the room to explore without an audience.

- **Backyard Sanctuary:** If you have access to a garden or a quiet space at home, begin there. It's the perfect place to practice forest bathing techniques without worrying about anyone watching what you're up to.

- **Off-Peak Hours:** If you're venturing into a public park, consider going early in the morning or later in the evening when it's quieter. These are the times when nature feels more peaceful, and you can enjoy the solitude, both in the natural world and from other people.

The goal is to find a space where you can let your guard down, allowing yourself to be fully present without the nagging worry of what others might think.

Finding Supportive Communities

Sometimes, all it takes to overcome self-consciousness is knowing that you're not the only one. Finding a community of like-minded people can help you feel more supported and less alone in your experience.

- **Social Media Groups:** There are online spaces dedicated to nature lovers and forest bathers, where you can connect with others who share your passion. These groups can be a great resource for tips, inspiration, and even organizing group outings.

- **Local Workshops:** Many environmental groups or parks offer forest bathing workshops and nature walks. These guided sessions can provide a reassuring introduction to the practice, and you'll be surrounded by others who are just as new to it as you are.

Letting Go of Perfection

I will say it again, forest bathing isn't about getting it right. It's not a class, and it's not a test. It's about connecting with nature in a way that feels genuine and comfortable for you. As a lifelong perfectionist, I'm proud to say that somewhere along the way I realized that the real magic in life comes from simply letting go of that need for perfection. The woods are full of surprises, and the more I relaxed, the more I noticed the beauty and peace around me. I don't need to know the names of all the insects and plants to be inspired by them.

So, the next time you head into the woods, leave the self-consciousness behind. Step in with curiosity and an open heart and let mother nature accept you exactly as you are. You will be surprised by what she shows you.

Obstacle 4 – "Is This Really Doing Anything?"

It's easy to question the impact of something so simple when life is full of noise and urgency. Walking through the trees, your mind might still be racing, wondering: "Is this really doing anything for me?" It's a valid question, especially when we're used to fast results and instant gratification. But the answer, backed by research and countless personal experiences, is a definite yes.

While the science shows us the broad benefits, your own experience is the most telling. Forest bathing is a personal practice, and the changes it brings may not always be immediate, but they are real. If it feels natural for you, why not track its effects by setting personal benchmarks to measure how it impacts you over time?

Creating Your Own Forest Bathing Journal

One lovely way to do this, is to keep a forest bathing or nature journal. Before each outing, jot down how you're feeling, both mentally and physically. After your time in the forest, take a moment to reflect on any changes. Even the smallest shifts can truly reveal how powerful nature's effect can be. Over time, you'll start to see patterns and connections between your time in nature and your overall well-being. Check out chapter 17 for ideas.

Patience and Consistency

Like any practice, the benefits of forest bathing don't always reveal themselves right away. Think of it as planting a tree: you don't see the roots grow on day one, but with consistent care, you know it will eventually flourish. Some days, you'll feel an immediate sense of calm, while other days might be quieter, more subtle. But over time, these experiences compound, and the impact on your mental and physical health becomes undeniable.

Testimonials and Stories

Sometimes, hearing others' stories can be just as powerful as experiencing it for yourself. Many people use forest bathing as a way to unwind from work, reconnect with loved ones, or even ease symptoms of anxiety or stress. Online, you'll find an array of stories about how time spent in nature has led to positive changes, from reduced stress levels to improved overall health.

Community stories are equally inspiring. If you're curious, it can be really lovely to seek them out – a quick search online can show you many experiences.

So, the next time you wonder, "Is this really doing anything for me?" consider the research, reflect on your own experiences, and listen to the voices of those who've been transformed by it. Forest bathing may not offer instant results, but over time, the changes in you will become more noticeable.

Obstacle 5 – "It's not Accessible for People Like Me"

Forest bathing is for everyone, regardless of physical ability. Nature's healing qualities are universal, and there are ways to make the practice more accessible to people with different needs.

Wheelchair-Friendly Nature Trails: Many parks and nature reserves now offer wheelchair-accessible trails. These well-maintained paths allow you to experience the forest without worrying about rough terrain. Check local maps or ask at visitor centres for accessible trail options.

Seated Forest Bathing: If mobility is limited, simply find a comfortable spot to sit, whether it's a bench, a chair, or even a blanket on the ground, and take in the sights, sounds, and scents around you. Let the forest come to you while you relax and connect.

Nature from Home: If getting out into the woods is challenging, virtual forest bathing is a wonderful alternative. With nature documentaries, live nature cams, or calming soundscapes, you can bring the forest into your living room. Even if you're not physically in the woods, these digital experiences offer a peaceful moment of connection. When I am back in the UK and missing Africa, I log on to the WildEarth channel on YouTube for either a sunrise or sunset safari streamed live from the game viewing vehicle from various locations across the continent. The marvel of modern technology can bring the wonders of the African bush direct to you in your own home.

Adapted Forest Bathing Techniques: Some people find peace in simply listening to the sounds of the forest or focusing on one specific scent. For those who are unable to explore far, try focusing on small, immediate details, like a leaf or a flower close to you, and let your attention rest there.

We've chatted through quite a few common hurdles here, and it's clear that, with a little tweak to our perspective and some simple adaptations, getting closer to nature is always within reach. And that idea of finding green when you feel utterly surrounded by concrete? That's such an important point, it truly deserves a whole chapter to itself. So, in the next chapter we'll really explore how to uncover those unexpected pockets of calm, even in the busiest city.

CHAPTER SEVEN

The Concrete Jungle

Discovering Nature in the City

Let's be honest: most of us aren't living at the edge of a pine forest. We're more likely to be surrounded by traffic, takeaway wrappers, and that one bloke who insists on having loud phone calls on public transport. But in these instances, nature hasn't left the building; she's just a little harder to find.

Finding Green in the Grey

Think of your city as a treasure map. Only instead of a big red X and a chest of gold, you're after patches of green, the kind that make your brain go "ahh" for a second.

Start with the parks. Even the small, unkempt ones with half a bench and a swing set with a squeaky chain. These places matter. They're the green lungs of the city, and your nervous system will thank you for spending time there.

Then there are greenways, those surprisingly magical strips of nature that run along old railway lines, canals, or cycle paths. You'd be surprised how much life is tucked in there if you slow down enough to notice it. Think of them as the city's hidden corridors, shortcuts to sanity. I once took a greenway shortcut that ended up adding 40 minutes to my journey because I kept stopping to admire unusual plants, fungi, and a particularly friendly magpie. Worth it.

Don't overlook the unexpected ones either – the rooftop gardens, the scrappy hedgerows behind bus stops, or even the well-kept flowerbeds outside registry offices. Designed for a nice wedding photo, yes, but perfectly good for a mindful sit too.

If it's green, it counts.

Urban Land Snorkelling

Land snorkelling isn't just for meandering a meadow or wandering a woodland. In the city, it's often just as rewarding. Walk slowly, eyes open, and you will spot the secrets hidden in the pavements, the walls, and garden fencing.

I've spotted ladybirds halfway up lampposts, poppies blooming out of cracked concrete, and once, a tiny frog trying to cross a bus lane. You don't need a forest, just curiosity and a willingness to look a little weird. It's the best kind of weird.

Not Just Steel and Glass

Despite their concrete appearance, cities are actually living, breathing ecosystems. And thankfully, some city planners have cottoned on. Green roofs, new parklets, tree-planting schemes – they're popping up everywhere.

It's worth poking around your council or city website now and again. You might discover that a grotty disused car park is about to become a wildflower meadow. (And if not, maybe you'll be the one who starts asking why not?)

Creatures of the Concrete Jungle

Think nature's left town? Tell that to the foxes that saunter past kebab shops at 2 am like they own the place. Or the peregrine falcons nesting on top of office blocks. Or the pigeons (yes, even them) who've somehow mastered surviving everything people throw at them.

There's biodiversity there, if you're paying attention. Trees lining streets. Insects in hanging baskets. Birds acting out full-scale soap opera fights on your windowsill.

Next time you're walking to the shop, switch on your nature-spotting brain. How many different species can you see before you get to the entrance? Maybe one day you pick birds, another you choose plants or insects.

Join the Green Team

You don't have to do it alone. Community gardens, local conservation groups, litter-picking gangs (yes, some are actually quite fun), they're all ways to connect more deeply with urban nature, and the people who care about it.

There's something deeply grounding about getting your hands in the soil, even if that soil is in a repurposed council planter behind a library.

So yes, the city's loud. It's messy. It's not always obvious where the green bits are. But they are there, hiding in plain sight, waiting for you to slow down and say hello.

Next time you're feeling hemmed in by the noise, go for a wander. Take the long route. Stop to really look at the moss on a wall. Watch the birds bicker in the branches. Try a bit of land snorkelling between meetings.

Balcony Bathing: Bringing the Forest to Your Urban Home

When the city's soundtrack never quite switches off – sirens, bin lorries, a neighbour who insists on karaoke at 2 am – your balcony, however small, can become a lifeline. A sort of "mini forest" in the sky. No passport, no wellies, no train fare. Just a quiet corner where you can feel a little more human again.

Creating a Green Oasis

You don't need a garden the size of Kew. You don't even need a garden. Even a bucket on a fire escape counts. A few planters and a willingness to potter can go a long way. The aim here isn't perfection, it's presence.

Pick pots that make you smile; terracotta if you like the earthy stuff, reclaimed tins if you're more retro and frugal. Compost still works whatever the container.

In the middle of city life, traffic humming, bins clattering, neighbours arguing over parking spaces, growing something green can be a real distraction. A tomato plant on the windowsill, a tray of seedlings on the balcony, a few pots that smell like summer when you brush past them. You're not escaping the urban sprawl; you're softening its edges. And when you grow and tend plants regularly, you end up crouched in a quiet bubble of concentration, inspecting new leaves and checking for greenfly. You start paying attention. To the weather. The soil. Whether your rosemary's looking a bit peaky or just having a bad day.

Plants that pull their weight:

Go for tough-but-lovely ones that don't sulk if you forget to water them occasionally. Think herbs like thyme and rosemary (practical, smells nice, tastes better), ferns for that "ancient woodland" vibe, or cheerful geraniums that are hard to kill off.

If you're new to this, don't overthink it. One pot. A bit of soil. Some seeds or a plant that makes you curious. Go from there. No fancy tools required. No five-year landscaping plan. Just enough interest to keep checking back and see what's changed. Hardy herbs like mint, thyme, or parsley are good first companions. They'll forgive a bit of neglect and come back swinging.

It's funny how much calm can come from something as low-key as deadheading a geranium or watering a pot of lettuce. The hands get busy, and the brain takes a breather. There's a rhythm to it, and your body seems to remember it, even if your last brush with gardening was growing cress on kitchen roll at school.

And when something you've planted thrives, or you spot a bee nosing into a flower you grew, there's this small, solid joy that comes with it. Quiet. But real.

The act of planting something and really looking after it also teaches patience. It reminds us that sometimes, just turning up every day and watering things (including yourself) is the work. You'll learn as you go, and if you don't, the plants will teach you anyway.

Short on space? Go up.

Balcony railings, walls, the back of your door – they're all fair game. Climbing plants like jasmine or honeysuckle will make the place smell amazing and look like you've moved into a tiny urban jungle.

Water's worth the effort:

Even a mini tabletop fountain or a shallow bowl with floating petals can shift the mood. Something about the sound of water tells your nervous system it's okay to unclench.

Bonus points:

Hanging baskets. Lanterns. A wind chime made from old keys. Basically, anything that reminds you this is your space, your haven, your patch of peace.

Sensory Stuff

The more senses you bring in, the more your little sanctuary will feel alive. Scented plants like lavender or night-scented stock. Textures you want to reach out and touch. Sounds that make you breathe a little deeper, whether it's real birdsong or a cheeky playlist of forest sounds in stereo.

And food for the senses isn't just for you. Hang a feeder or grow something pollinator-friendly and wait for the bees to show up. You might even get a robin who decides it's their balcony now.

Your Sit Spot in the Sky

This doesn't have to be all Instagram-ready and perfect. Just... sit. Let the coffee go cold. Watch what the light does. Make a small ritual of it, a daily check-in with your balcony, your mood, your weather. Keep a little notebook if that's your thing, (or whisper notes into your phone like a slightly eccentric nature detective)... What direction does the moon rise? How does the sun shift? Did that spider always have only seven legs or is something going on? You'll be amazed what you spot when you actually look.

Growing Together

If space is really not available or you just fancy some company, community gardens are worth seeking out. They've got that mix of shared purpose and friendly chaos, people helping each other out, swapping tips and seedlings, forgetting each other's names but remembering the size of each other's onions. You'll come away with dirt under your nails, a few new skills, and possibly more courgettes than you know what to do with. Chapter 15 **explores** this a little deeper.

Once you start forest bathing, even if it's just from your balcony jungle or a corner of the local park, doing it regularly means you'll begin to notice things you used to breeze past. The way the air smells different. The leaves that looked green yesterday now tinged with gold. A bird call you haven't heard in a while.

Without trying, you start tuning into the rhythm of the seasons. It's like your body remembers something it always knew, but forgot in the rush.

In the next chapter, we'll follow that rhythm, from winter stillness to summer hum, and look at how forest bathing shifts as the wheel of the year turns.

CHAPTER EIGHT

Through the Seasons

Spring: Renewal and Growth

Noticing New Life

Spring is an odd one for me. We often talk of it with words like "bursting into life," which suggests a grand, confident entrance, but for me, it's nothing like that, well not at the start anyway. One day, the sun teases you with glorious warmth, and the next, you're pulling your woollies back out. It's truly a stop-start season, my pot plants certainly know the drill, getting shuttled in and out of the house daily for fear of an unexpected frost!

But this unpredictable rhythm also makes the genuine signs of new life all the more precious. The forest starts its slow reveal, from tiny snowdrops elbowing through crisp leaf litter, to brave crocuses, then a whole chorus of things tentatively waking up and stretching toward the sun. Look for buds fattening, catkins dangling, and blossom that just wasn't there yesterday. Mornings and evenings are especially lovely; low light, long shadows, and that gorgeous, vivid lime green that pops against the still-bare branches. Worth pausing for, indeed.

Dawn Chorus

In springtime, the bird song is at its absolute loudest. Every avian from miles around shouting "I'm here!", "This is my patch!", "Looking for a mate!", or sometimes, simply "I made it through the night!". And what a wonderful time to truly listen, to tune in and maybe even learn a few different bird songs and calls. Not only are they all singing their hearts out (many go quiet by late summer, or migrate), but with the trees still mostly bare, birds are much easier to see and identify.

There are some fantastic apps for your smartphone that identify bird calls for you, and they're brilliant for quickly checking a sound or when a bird is simply too hidden by foliage to see clearly. But for me, the joy is in the challenge of truly listening for a call, and then patiently trying to track it to find the bird. That bit of detective work, that small 'investment' of time and curiosity, seems to root the bird and its song much more firmly in my mind, way more so than an instant answer from an app ever could.

Spring Showers

There's something about spring rain that feels... helpful. Less of a soaking, more of a rinse. It's the kind of rain that brings out colour and smell; earth, moss, bark, flowers, all turning the volume up just a notch after a spring shower.

If you're out walking at dawn or dusk after a few days of rain, keep an eye out for barn owls. They tend to hunt over open fields and meadows, pinpointing mice and voles in the grass with their exceptional hearing. However, they cannot hunt in heavy rain (the rain impairs their hearing and their feathers are structured in a way that ensures silent flight, but means that they cannot get them too wet). As you can imagine, owls are therefore pretty hungry after a few days of rain and so they tend to stay out hunting for longer into the daylight hours increasing your chances of seeing them, especially if they have young to feed.

Mindful Foraging

If you're someone who likes to nibble on the seasons, spring has loads to offer after the barren winter; wild garlic, young nettles, maybe some cleavers clinging to your socks. Young hawthorn and beech leaves, hazel catkins and dandelions. But remember this isn't a supermarket aisle; so pick with care. Leave plenty. Learn what's what before you eat anything. And if you're not sure? Leave it be. Curiosity is good; poisoning yourself is less ideal.

Journaling or Photography

Spring is sneaky. One day the forest looks bare, the next it's an explosion of life. Taking photos or jotting notes can help you slow down enough to truly *see* it and not miss it completely.

Look for contrast, last year's decay next to this year's new shoots. A frostbitten log with moss pushing through. That one tree that's gone full green while its neighbour is still snoozing.

As you slow down to notice all this awakening around you, you might find something stirring within yourself too. Spring's new growth isn't just for the plants and trees after all. If you're pondering what this season might mean for you, perhaps these thoughts can guide your journaling or simply spark a quiet reflection:

1. **What's waking up in you right now?** Just as the earth begins to stir with renewed energy, you might notice new interests or forgotten ideas gently pushing their way to the surface within you. Is there a spark of creativity you haven't felt for a while? A gentle shift in perspective, or perhaps a new curiosity emerging? Pay attention to those subtle internal stirrings, much like watching for the first tentative buds on a tree.

2. **What are you itching to grow or change within yourself?** Spring is a natural time for growth, and that applies to us just as much as it does to the natural world. Perhaps there's a small new habit you'd like to cultivate, or a fresh way of being you'd like to bring into your days. What qualities within you are ready to reach for the light?

3. **What hopes and aspirations do you have for the season?** With the days stretching longer and a wonderful sense of fresh possibility in the air, what kind of energy do you want to invite into your life for the coming months? What seeds of intention would you like to plant for yourself? Think broadly. Perhaps it's more quiet outdoor moments, more laughter-filled connections with others, or simply a deeper sense of presence in your everyday.

Just let your thoughts unfurl naturally, guided by the green world around you.

Summer: Full Tilt Forest

Summer in the woods is thick and bushy. The trees are heavy, the air hums with insects, and everything seems to stretch; time, light, limbs. The forest feels expansive, like it's exhaling after months of holding itself in. This is the season of lazy walks, naps in shade, and checking your drinks glass for wasps.

Talking of wasps, before you flinch or reach for the swatter, take a breath and consider this...

Some wasps are master potters, others are gardeners, and a few are massively misunderstood heroes of the hedgerow. Of the 9000 species recorded in Britain, here are a few common wasps you're likely to encounter in England;

Potter Wasp (*Eumenes spp.*)

- Sleek, reddish or black, often alone and zipping about walls or wooden posts.

- These solitary wasps build miniature mud pots to house their eggs. Each pot is stocked with a paralysed caterpillar so that their young when hatched have fresh food to eat! They're pest control with wings.

Common Wasp (*Vespula vulgaris*) / German Wasp (*Vespula germanica*)

- These two are almost identical apart from some tiny marking differences too small to worry about – basically they have bright yellow-and-black stripes, medium size, often the fizzy-drink-loiterer.

- These social wasps are expert foragers and help clean up decaying matter. They are tiny janitors.

- Highly adaptable and can been spotted using chewed wood to build nests on fences, in sheds and loft spaces.

Tree Wasp (*Dolichovespula sylvestris*)
- Slightly larger with a long solid yellow face, dark with subtle markings, often nesting in tree hollows.

- Despite looking intense, they're shy and rarely sting unless provoked.

European Hornet (*Vespa crabro*)
- Enormous and golden-brown, with a hum that turns heads.

- Though intimidating, they're gentle giants, less aggressive than their smaller cousins and largely ignore humans unless threatened.

Instead of seeing a blur of panic with wings, what if we saw wasps as the tiny engineers, hunters, and recyclers that they are? They pollinate, manage garden pests, and keep ecosystems in balance, there'd be way more aphids in my garden without wasps. Maybe next time one hovers by your sandwich, you'll pause, observe the markings, and marvel at its purpose and position at the top of its' food chain.

Incidentally if you spot a Yellow-Legged (aka Asian) Hornet, please report it immediately! These hornets are a significant threat to our native honeybees and other vital pollinators, and they can spread incredibly quickly. Early reporting is absolutely crucial, as it gives our fantastic wildlife organisations the best chance to find and manage nests before they become widely established and cause serious damage to our delicate ecosystems. You can report sightings here:

https://risc.brc.ac.uk/alert.php?species=asian_hornet

Version 6. Produced by Lucy Cornwell, Olaf Booy (NNSS), Gay Marris, Mike Brown (National Bee Unit) with assistance from Colette O'Flynn (National Biodiversity Data Centre Ireland) Stuart Roberts (BWARS)

Leaning Into the Light

The longest day of the year arrives at the solstice around the third week of June in the northern hemisphere. Where I live, that means a 4am dawn and a 10pm dusk – long evenings, hours of that perfect low golden sunlight that photographers love so much. You don't have to do anything special, just noticing it is enough.

Ideas for solstice-ish moments:

- Catch a sunrise if you're up early (or haven't gone to bed yet). Begin the day with a slow, sensory walk through woodland at sunrise. Pause beneath trees, breathe in the scent of summer leaves. You might even write a few words on leaves or stones and place them along your path. End with a simple tea ceremony using wild herbs like elderflower or watermint.

- Linger in a meadow with a flask and a snack. Let yourself lie down in the grass for longer than feels productive. Bring a singing bowl, chimes, or even a playlist of soft nature sounds. Let the vibrations blend with birdsong for a meditative immersion.

- Create a Nature Mandala. Gather petals, leaves, stones, and twigs to form a sun-shaped mandala on the forest floor. It's a quiet, creative way to honour the turning of the year and leave a gentle offering to the land.

It's not about squeezing the most out of the day. It's about letting the day stretch you. Take your notebook and write with the sun on your skin. Try prompts like: *"What is ready to shine more brightly in my life?"* or *"What am I ready to release with the setting sun?"*

Water: The Good Kind of Distraction

In the heat, water is where everything congregates; birds, insects, overheated people. A shaded stream or mossy pond is basically summer's version of a chill-out zone.

Things to try:

- Trail your fingers in the current and see what floats by.

- Sit near moving water and let it do that background-noise thing brains seem to like.

- If it's clean and safe, take a dip. Only needs to be a few minutes, just long enough to reset your body temperature and your brain.

Staying Comfortable

Yes, summer is glorious. It also bites. Literally. But don't let that put you off. A little planning keeps you in the moment, not swatting, scratching or dehydrated.

Basics:

- Water bottle. Always. More than you think you need.

- Light layers to keep midges out and sunburn at bay.

- Quick tick check when you get home, boring but worth it.

Summer in the forest is rich, rowdy, and full of life. Whether you're ambling under the trees, snoozing in a meadow, or standing ankle-deep in a stream wondering where your sandal went, the season's big message is clear: take up space, stretch out, and let yourself enjoy it.

Autumnal Reflections: Letting Go with the Falling Leaves

Autumn is when the forest really shows off. One last burst of brilliance before everything quietens down. The trees throw a full-blown colour party and go out in style during autumn, and honestly, this is my favourite season. You get to cosy up, eat everything you've grown, switch the salads for soups and stews, light bonfires, and come home with a red nose, wind-swept hair and that smug 'I've been outside' feeling.

The showy flowers might be over, but there's still plenty going on. Acorns thump to the ground, fungi poke their heads through damp leaf litter, and squirrels get seriously intense about their food stashes. The forest is busy in its own scruffy, unfocused way.

Watch how the animals prepare. We all spot the squirrels burying their treasure, but look a little closer, and you'll see so much more going on.

Think about the trees, for instance. When the leaves turn yellow, the trees are actually pulling all that goodness, all the chlorophyll, back into their trunks and roots, letting the leaves go. Those leaves then become a cosy blanket and food for the soil, recycling nutrients beautifully. Many other plants are busy making and dropping their last seeds, ready for next spring, or offering up a final, rich feast of berries and nuts for the animals. Perennials are sending all their energy down to their roots, preparing to hunker down underground for the winter.

And the animals! Our resident birds like robins and tits are busy fattening up, storing energy, while you might spot jays carefully burying acorns for later, they're remarkably clever at remembering where they've put them! If you're lucky, you'll see flocks of swallows gathering on power lines, chattering excitedly as they prepare for their long journey south. And keep an eye out for the first redwings and fieldfares arriving from colder climes, ready to feast on our autumn berries. Down on the ground, hedgehogs are on a serious mission to pile on the pounds, munching on as many slugs and worms as they can find, getting ready for their big winter sleep. Even the tiny world of insects is busy with preparation. Look closely under bark or in sheltered crevices, and you might find queen wasps or bumblebees seeking out a safe spot to hibernate until spring. Ladybirds often gather in surprisingly large groups to huddle together for warmth, sometimes even finding their way into our sheds or window frames.

It really is quite a show of industry, this whole autumn getting-ready phase. Every rustle of leaves, every hurried scurry, is part of that deep, instinctive preparation. So next time you're out amongst the turning leaves, listen for that busy hum, watch for the determined foraging, and just let yourself be drawn into all the clever preparations unfolding around you.

The Colours of Change

Green gives way to a riot of amber, crimson, rust and gold. Colours that only stick around for a few days. Each tree is doing its own thing; maples going scarlet, birches catching the light like they're made of silver foil, oaks turning that deep, proper autumn brown. It's not subtle, and that's the point. Autumn isn't about restraint.

What to do to mark the Autumn equinox, a time of balance...

- A lot of people like to gather smooth stones and stack them in small cairns in a stream or along your path to acknowledge balance, but I would like to gently discourage this. Whilst it's not illegal here in the UK, it does tend to disturb fragile eco-systems and goes against the principle of *"leave no trace"*. So whilst its great to do it in your own garden with your own pebbles, please refrain from doing it elsewhere and especially do not take pebbles or shells etc. from the beach as that definitely *is* illegal in the UK – it's considered coastal erosion and carries a hefty fine!

- Write something you're ready to let go of on a fallen leaf; an old habit, a fear, a lingering sadness. Then release it into a stream or let the wind carry it away. A simple, symbolic act of seasonal shedding. Think about what's falling away in your own life. Some things aren't meant to be carried through the winter.

- Create a small altar with conkers, rose hips, dried grasses, and seed pods. Maybe add a note of intention for the season ahead, or a candle if using a windowsill arrangement at home.

- Autumn is prime time for mushrooms. Bring a small sketchbook and draw the ones you find. No need to identify them, just observe their shapes and colours. It's a meditative way to connect with and marvel at the forest's underground communications network.

- Find a quiet spot in the woods during the golden hour and write with the fading light. This is the season where you get to look back at your own effort, too. What have you grown? Made? Got through? Try prompts like: "What am I harvesting from this year so far?" or "What inner light do I want to carry into the darker months?"

- Practice alternate nostril breathing (*nadi shodhana*). This simple technique is known to harmonize the left and right hemispheres of the brain, symbolically and physically restoring equilibrium.

> *"There's no such thing as bad weather, only bad clothing"*

If it's raining, don't let that stop you. Pull on your waterproofs and wellies, you'll meet fewer people and more of the forest. I tend to stay out longer when I'm wearing waterproof trousers as well as a jacket; you're simply more willing to sit on the damp earth when you know you won't be going home in soggy jeans.

Being warm and dry means you're more open to the moment. You're more likely to notice the intricate beads of rain clinging to a leaf, and less likely to sulk because your socks are wet.

Collecting Fallen Leaves

> *"All the leaves are losing their leaves and not one of them is worried"* – **Donald Miller**

Letting go is both graceful and essential.

I press a lot of leaves in autumn. Some to decorate my jewellery stall[1], some just because they're beautiful. There's something calming about choosing a leaf, knowing it's done is job and is heading down to nourish the earth, serving its next important purpose.

Ideas:

- Look for the ones with character; freckles, holes, strange edges. The perfect ones are fine, but the wonky ones have stories.

- Press them in a heavy book, make leaf mandalas, or just hold one for a minute and breathe.

Autumn is the season of sorting, clearing, savouring. It says: *You made it through the growing part. Now slow down. Rest a bit. Eat the soup.* And I, for one, am absolutely up for that.

Winter Wonders: Finding Stillness and Clarity Amongst the Bare Trees

That pull towards the cosy sofa, a warm cuppa, and fluffy slippers when the wind howls outside is incredibly strong, isn't it? Believe me, I feel it too – the temptation to just hibernate until spring rolls around is real for so many of us. The temperature has dropped considerably since last season and the squidgey mud has frozen all paw prints into solid icy bumps, slippy and treacherous. Why would we want to venture out into that?

The trees have stripped back to the essentials, the air has that sharp, nose-tingling clarity, and everything slows right down. It's not lifeless, it's just on pause. That kind of stillness does something to your brain. Calms the fidgets. Clears the noise.

---

1. https://elementalretail.com/jewellery/

In winter, the woodland settles into a different kind of beauty, one that's quiet but expectant. It's a stark, honest loveliness that is here for a precious, short time. To truly make the most of the few hours of daylight during winter we need to leave the sofa behind and step onto that frosty path.

If you're holding out for the perfect weather before heading out, you'll miss half the charm. Sun, rain, snow, fog; the forest always has something to offer, and usually it's not what you expected (in a good way, mostly). The trick is to go anyway. Show up, even if the clouds look grim, just remember to pick a sheltered route if the wind's having a tantrum. No one enjoys being slapped in the face by a branch at sub-zero temperatures.

What to do?

Once you've peeled yourself off the sofa, wrapped up warm, and stepped into that brisk winter air, it's about knowing how to engage with the woodland in a way that truly speaks to the season's unique character.

One of the most rewarding things you can do is simply embrace the cold and the stillness. The woods appear to be in a deep, restorative sleep after the busy seasons of growth and harvest. Imagine the creatures nestled away, conserving energy. You can do a version of that yourself: find a quiet spot, maybe lean against a sturdy tree, and just be present in the quiet. Let your own busy thoughts quieten, just as the forest has. Should the cold begin to really nip at your nose, or perhaps your teeth start to chatter, don't feel you have to stay rooted to the spot. A gentle wander will soon get the blood flowing again, and as you move, try focusing on your breath. A few strong, warm exhalations can sometimes work wonders, reminding you of the incredible warmth you can generate from within.

While everything above ground might seem dormant, take a moment to look at the ground beneath the bare trees. Those soggy, matted leaves from last autumn? They're not just 'dead' in the way we often think; they're slowly, patiently breaking down. This is the forest's quiet work of replenishment, turning last season's bounty into the very food that will nourish the spring growth. Even in rest, something incredibly important is transforming and preparing for what comes next.

Winter, especially with a touch of frost or a dusting of snow across the fields, is the perfect time to become a woodland detective. Keep your eyes peeled for animal tracks. A robin's delicate hop, the purposeful stride of a deer, or the distinctive paw prints of a fox or badger can tell a tiny story of who has passed this way before you. Each print connects you to the hidden, often unseen, lives of the creatures around you. Try to follow a set of tracks for a bit, imagining the animal's journey and what they might have been up to.

With fewer leaves to block the view, the winter sky often feels vast and dramatic. On a day with crisp, clear air, or when those heavy, dramatic snow clouds roll in, take some time to simply look up. Sometimes you'll see incredible formations, like huge, textured sculptures drifting overhead, or perhaps the softer, almost glowing clouds on a frosty morning. Let your mind find shapes and stories in them; it's a lovely, simple way to let your imagination roam freely.

And speaking of looking up, the bare trees themselves offer a masterclass in natural art. Without their leafy coats, their true structures are revealed. Take a moment to study the silhouettes of the trees against a pale or dramatic sky. Look at the intricate network of branches, the unique outline of an oak, or the delicate wisps of a birch. Each species has its own distinctive shape, a sort of winter signature. Notice how they give each other space, and stand tall, even when exposed to the elements, a real picture of consideration and strength.

Winter As a Mental Rest and Reset

This is the season for paring things back. Fewer plans. Slower days. Hot drinks in forgotten flasks. Sit on a log. Lean on a tree. Let your shoulders drop.

You can bring a journal, but honestly, a thousand-yard-stare into the middle distance works just as well. Let your brain breathe. Let winter teach you how to rest without guilt, or at least stop trying so hard. And yes, heated socks count as one of modern life's tiny triumphs.

Winter is still and stark, beautiful in a way that asks for nothing. Whether you are tracing pawprints, wrapped in too many layers, or standing in a silent wood wondering where the year went, it holds space for you.

It may take a little extra resolve to pull on those layers and step outside when the world feels so still and cold. But once you do, winter offers gifts you will not find in any other season. Think of the low light painting bare branches in soft gold and cool grey. Familiar paths become quietly magical. There is a deep peace in the woods when nature rests, a hush that feels both ancient and comforting. Seeing the trees simply stand through the weather is steadying.

Once your boots are laced, there is the question of company. Is it just you and the trees, or will there be other humans too? Some people crave quiet solitude. Others would not dream of heading out without a friend, or at least someone to blame if they get lost. So, do you head out solo, or turn it into a woodland social with snacks?

Chapter Nine

Solo vs Shared

Wandering Alone or With Company

O nce you're kitted out and ready to face whatever the weather's throwing out, there's another decision waiting: do you head into the forest on your own, or bring someone (or several someones) along for the ride?

I've tried it all; wandering solo, walking with kids, old friends, new friends, dogs, distracted toddlers, and once even a group of lively retirees who could outpace me uphill without breaking a sweat. And honestly? Every version brings something different. But the one thing they all have in common: I never regret it. I always leave the woods feeling more human. More grounded. Slightly muddier.

Wandering Alone

There's something special about having the forest to yourself. It's just you and the trees, and maybe a curious robin keeping an eye on you. You get to sink into your own rhythm. There's no need to talk, no one asking what time lunch is, just space to breathe, to think, to notice the small things like the way a shaft of sunlight lands exactly on that one fern, or how the wind makes the branches creak against each other making odd noises.

Solo walks are when I tend to untangle thoughts I didn't even realise were knotted. No pressure to perform, no small talk, just me and the path.

The Joys of Company

That said, forest bathing with others has its own kind of magic. Everything gets lifted a little. There's laughter echoing off the trees, shared wonder at spotting a deer or a weird-looking fungus, and maybe even a group sigh of relief when someone breaks out the biscuits.

I remember a camping trip in Sussex years ago, one of those spontaneous climbs where we all decided to hike up the hill "just to see the view." We reached the top, cracked open a few drinks, tried to revive a struggling bumblebee with sugar water, and took a lot of very questionable photos. We laughed all the way back down and kept laughing around the campfire until late. That kind of shared memory sticks.

The Middle Ground: Walking With Strangers

Joining a group walk with people you don't know can be a bit of a wild card, but I've had some really lovely experiences that way. ou never know what stories might emerge or what new insights someone could share. What's more, there's a surprising sense of freedom in walking with people who don't know you – no old expectations, no need to perform, just the chance to simply be yourself.

Make It Yours

When you do walk with others, it doesn't need to be a big organised event. Some of the best moments happen naturally: a pause at a viewpoint, a shared grin at a muddy mishap, or that unspoken agreement to just *be quiet* for a bit.

You could try:

- **Silent walking:** No pressure, just a few minutes of companionable quiet. See what you notice.

- **Mindful chats:** Keep the conversation light and rooted in the surroundings. "Did you hear that woodpecker?" is better than "So how's work going?"

- **End-of-walk sharing:** If you're with a small group, it can be surprisingly lovely to sit in a circle and each name one thing that stood out.

- **Journaling afterwards:** Whether you walked alone or with company, note down what felt good. It helps anchor the experience.

Some years ago, I decided to walk the length of the South Downs Way; a long-distance trail across southern England, all rolling hills, chalk paths, and wide skies. For much of it, I walked alone, and it suited me fine. I settled into a steady rhythm, finding a strange kind of conversation with the land itself. The rise and fall of hills, the padded short grass underfoot, the sudden heart-lifting view when you crest a ridge. Stunning.

But somewhere along the way, I fell into step with a stranger: an older man, wiry and sun-browned, who introduced himself as a retired army major. We struck up a casual conversation, the kind you have when there's no real pressure to be interesting or impressive.

At some point, as we tackled yet another seemingly endless incline, he quietly offered a few tips on hill walking. Things I'd somehow missed in 50-odd years of stomping around the countryside. Simple things like adjusting my posture, and lengthening my stride by just an inch or so.

It sounded almost laughably minor.
One inch? What difference could that possibly make?

Turns out, quite a lot. Over the course of a long day, and an even longer trail, that tiny adjustment saved me untold amounts of energy. I felt it immediately in my legs and in my breathing. Hills that had felt like the longest slog suddenly became manageable. Not easy, exactly, but no longer punishing.

I don't remember his name.
I remember his kindness.
I remember the feeling of learning something I didn't even know I needed to learn.
And I remember thinking: sometimes, nature teaches you through other people.

Solitude and shared moments each have their place. Some days, you'll want to walk alone. Some days, the presence of another, whether they're a friend, a fellow forest bather, or a chatty ex-military hill-climbing coach, might be exactly what you need. Both are valid. Both are valuable.

In the end, it's not really about whether you go solo or with others, it's about what you need that day. Some days call for stillness and introspection. Others call for a shared thermos of tea and someone to laugh with when you slip in the mud. Other times you need a stranger to remind you that a small change, a shift so slight you can hardly see it, can make all the difference.

The forest is generous. However you show up, it offers something in return.

And then there's the night.

Walking in the forest after dark is a whole different thing, moodier, quieter, and honestly, a bit thrilling. That's where walking with others can really come into its own. There's safety in numbers, yes, but also a kind of shared awe in stepping into the hush of the woods after the sun's gone down. You notice different things in the dark. Sounds seem louder, shadows stretch deeper, and your senses wake up in new ways. If the idea of forest bathing by moonlight makes you curious (or a little nervous), you're not alone. Let's go there next.

Chapter Ten

After Dark

After Hours: Forest Bathing in the Dark

The idea of wandering into the woods after sunset might sound a bit daft at first, like the start of a horror film or a questionable team-building exercise. But honestly? It's one of my favourite ways to experience a woodland. The forest changes at night. It's quieter, stiller, and yes, just a bit spookier.

Let's be clear though, it's not all mystical moonbeams and owl calls. Sometimes it's accidentally walking into a spiderweb, swearing loudly, then pretending you were just startled by the majesty of the trees. Or mistaking a molehill for a hedgehog and gently whispering "hello little guy" to a clump of dirt. It happens.

What's Different After Dark?

- **Your brain goes a bit bonkers.** Without light, your imagination cranks up to full power. That rustle in the brambles? Definitely not a squirrel, probably a serial killer deer. The silhouette ahead? Could be a tree. Could be Bigfoot. Who knows.

- **Your senses get dramatic.** You hear *everything*. Twigs snapping, leaves shifting, your own breath. You smell damp earth, wet bark, and possibly your own panic sweat.

- **Time slows down.** Not in a poetic way. More in a "how is it only 8:15?" kind of way.

Top Tips for Not Losing Your Mind (or Your Footing)

- **Go with friends.** You'll feel less daft, and laughter makes the strange noises feel less spooky.

- **Head torch = safety net.** But try switching it off now and again and let your eyes do their thing. They can handle more than you think, and it adds so much to the atmosphere. Just give them a good ten or fifteen minutes to really adjust before you set off – you'll feel them start pulling subtle shapes and then surprising outlines from the inky blackness. Just mind the dead logs!

- **Stick to well-known routes.** This is not the time to "see where this path goes."

- **Wear proper shoes.** Dew + uneven ground + sandals = comedy fall waiting to happen.

- **Expect the unexpected.** Like tripping over a tree root, hearing frogs in surround sound, or discovering just how loud an owl can be when it's right above your head.

Moments You Won't Forget

One of my all-time favourites was a night walk with friends during which one of them shrieked ridiculously loudly because something brushed her leg, it turned out to be her own scarf caught in the breeze. We still remind her about it, often. The walk ended with us lying on our backs in the grass, watching the stars while one of the group tried to identify constellations and just made them up: "That one's The Goat. And that's… Steve." We had no idea what we were looking at, but it didn't matter.

Stargazing in the Glade

There's something deeply grounding about lying in an open woodland glade, especially on a clear night. The air cools, the trees frame the edges of the sky like a natural planetarium, and suddenly you're not looking at the stars, you're in them.

I do this a lot when I'm in Africa. Out there, with zero light pollution and a horizon that stretches for miles, the night sky feels enormous. Not just big. *Enormous.* Like it could tip over and spill stars all over you. You can actually see the Milky Way, clear as anything. Not just a twinkle here and there, but layers upon layers of stars, like someone shook glitter across a vast velvet cloth. You stop thinking about emails and dinner plans. You just... float. It's oddly freeing to feel so tiny.

One star I always look for is Sirius, the Dog Star. Not just because it's bright (though it is, it's the brightest in the night sky), but because I once read it resonates at the same frequency as Earth. Whether that's *technically* true or more of a poetic rumour, I don't actually care. I love the idea that it hums a tune that matches our own.

It reminds me of an acoustics test I heard about... if you strike a G note on a piano at one end of a room, the G string on a guitar leaning against the wall at the other might vibrate too, just quietly. Same note, same frequency, bouncing through the space between. I find that oddly comforting, that something so far away, seemingly disconnected, could still make something here respond. So maybe, just maybe, lying still under a sky full of stars, you're picking up the cosmic version of that. A vibration. A whisper. A constant signal to us that we're part of something much bigger, even if we don't fully understand it yet.

Bonus tip: Time it with a meteor shower.
The Perseids are a good one to watch for in the British summer, mid-August usually, and they're bright, frequent, and incredibly satisfying to spot. Other showers pop up through the year too. Look up the dates, mark your calendar, and if the sky's clear, just go. There's something about seeing streaks of light tearing across the sky that makes you gasp out loud like a kid again. Not only that, it connects you with something ancient. The stars we see now are the same ones that lit up our ancestors' lives.

Why Bother Heading Out After Dark?

Because the forest at night has a kind of quiet you just don't get during the day. It pulls your attention outwards, away from phone screens and to-do lists, and into the world right in front of you. Your body comes alive and your senses tune in. Once you get used to it, there's a strange kind of calm in walking through the dark and realising you're not scared, you're actually peaceful. Even when you *are* scared, it's often just your brain making shapes in the shadows.

So go on, grab a friend, a torch, and a healthy sense of humour, and give it a go. The woods are waiting, and they've seen far sillier things than you.

CHAPTER ELEVEN

Yoga & Meditation

Mindfulness Meets the Great Outdoors

When you hear words like 'yoga' or 'meditation', your mind might immediately conjure images of super bendy people on mats, or gurus sitting cross-legged for hours, looking incredibly serene. And if that's not you – if the idea of touching your toes feels like a major life goal, or your brain refuses to be quiet for more than thirty seconds – it's easy to think this chapter might not be for you. But hold on a moment! I'm not here to turn you into a fully-fledged yogi, nor am I suggesting you spend your entire day contemplating your navel. What I do believe, though, is that everyone, regardless of their flexibility or experience, could find a real benefit from just a few simple stretches each day, and a moment or two of quiet calm. It's about finding tiny pockets of mindful movement and stillness that can make a surprisingly big difference to how you feel, to your mobility and especially when you do it out amongst the trees.

Yoga in the Forest

I spent some time a while back helping out friends at a Zambian safari lodge[1] Their stunning camp sat right on the banks of the Kafue river with its noisy hippos, secretive crocodiles and majestic elephants meandering past. It was a magical place to stay and I was fortunate enough to arrive a few days before the owner was hosting a yoga retreat for half a dozen ladies from around the country. What a treat, balancing on ancient rocks, just metres from the fast flowing waters. The sunrise warming the stone beneath our feet and sparkling brightly on the water rushing past, balanced by the ever present awareness that wildlife might be watching of course. Listening to exotic bird sounds and breathing in the clear African air made it a yoga session that will be very hard to forget, let alone beat! But you don't need to go to such extremes to feel the benefit of woodland yoga...

- **Finding Your Spot:** Pick a flat-ish patch where you can set up without disrupting the local residents, no one likes a beetle up your bum or ants in your pants. Open spaces or areas near a stream work well for both your balance and your view.

---

1. https://kasabushi.com/

- **Going with the Flow:** The forest isn't a yoga studio, and that's the beauty of it. A tree pose feels more grounded next to an actual tree, and those wobbles on uneven ground? That's just your body getting a lesson in focus.

- **Using Nature's Props:** Forget fancy blocks and straps. A sturdy log can help with balance, a smooth stone can give a stretch some weight, and a sloped patch of grass can turn a forward fold into a gravity-assisted masterpiece.

Not a Yogi? No Worries! Simple Ways to Stretch in the Forest

If the thought of 'downward dog' brings on a mild panic, then this bit's for you. You absolutely don't need to be a seasoned yogi to find incredible benefit from a little mindful movement in the woods. Think of these less as formal 'poses' and more as gentle ways to loosen up your body, clear your head, and simply feel a bit more comfortable in your skin. No one's judging; the trees certainly aren't!

Reach for the Sky: Imagine you're trying to tickle the lowest cloud, or stretch up to reach a really high branch. Start by simply reaching both arms up towards the canopy, lengthening your whole body. Then, gently try reaching one arm a little higher, then the other, almost like a slow, sleepy morning stretch. You'll feel it opening up your sides and giving your spine a lovely wake-up call. It's a simple way to feel taller and more open to the world around you.

Side Stretches for Space: Sometimes, you just need a bit more room to breathe. With your arms still overhead, take hold of one wrist and gently pull it over to the opposite side, leaning your body gently into the stretch. You're aiming for a lovely lengthening sensation all along your side, from your hip right up to your fingertips. Take a slow breath here, feeling the space you're creating. Then swap sides, move like the unfurling of new bracken.

Gentle Forward Fold: This is just about letting go. Stand with your feet about hip-width apart, and gently hinge forward from your hips, letting your head hang heavy towards the ground. You don't need to touch your toes, you don't even need to keep your legs straight, just go as far as feels comfortable. Let your arms dangle or rest your hands on your thighs. Imagine melting towards the earth, letting go of any tension in your back or shoulders. It's surprisingly calming.

Open Your Chest, Open Your Heart: If you spend a lot of time hunched over a desk or phone, this one feels wonderful. Take your hands behind your back and try to interlace your fingers (if that's comfortable). If not, simply open your arms wide like you're trying to hug a really enormous tree, letting your chest expand. Lift your sternum gently towards the sky. It's a beautiful way to counteract that forward-leaning posture and invite more of the fresh air in.

Ancient Footsteps: Creating Your Own Meditative Loop

I remember reading about how, long ago, people would use carefully laid out paths, sometimes intricate mazes, sometimes just simple circles, in sacred groves for meditation. The whole idea wasn't about getting to the middle or finishing first; it was about the simple act of putting one foot in front of the other. That gentle, repetitive motion was a powerful way to quiet the busy mind and turn focus inwards. It was a kind of walking prayer, or a way to untangle thoughts without even realising it.

Now, most of us don't have access to a perfectly manicured turf labyrinth or ancient grove in our local woods, and that's perfectly fine. We can easily borrow the spirit of that practice and make it our own.

- **Find Your Spot:** Look for a clear, short loop or circuit. Maybe it's a hundred-metre path that curves gently back to where you started, or even just a particularly appealing stands of trees that you can walk around a few times. If there's no clear loop, a short, straight stretch of path that you walk back and forth along for a few minutes can work just as well. The beauty isn't in the length or the grandeur of the path; it's in the repetition.

- **Focus Your Attention:** As you walk your chosen circuit, gently bring your attention to your feet on the ground. Feel the rise and fall of the earth beneath you, the gentle sway of your body. Notice your breath, just the natural rhythm of it, without trying to change it. Count your steps, are they the same for each circuit? Can you make them the same?

- **Engage Your Senses:** Let your gaze soften. What do you see in your immediate vicinity? What do you hear? The crunch of leaves or frost, the distant birdsong, the hum of unseen insects? The subtle scent of damp earth or pine needles? The repetition of the path helps your mind let go of distractions, allowing these small details to come into sharper focus, pulling you deeper into the present moment.

It's surprisingly powerful, this simple repetitive act. The world is constantly pushing us to go faster and achieve more, but intentionally choosing a small path and walking it slowly and mindfully, can be a profound way to resist and rebel.

Nature as Your Guide

At the heart of forest meditation and yoga is a deep respect for what's around you. The natural world is everyone's habitat. The line between "us" and "nature" is always thinner than we think. We *are* nature.

- **Life Force Reflections:** Think of the energy flowing through you and the forest, it's all part of the same thing. The same life force powering the oak tree is keeping your heart beating too. (You're basically related.)

- **Noticing Interconnectedness:** Forests are the original community builders, plants, animals, fungi, bacteria all working together. We're not lone wolves, however much we might pretend otherwise.

I remember sitting beside a river once, entirely silent, captivated by a single leaf that had just fallen from a nearby tree. It drifted down, landed softly on the water in front of me, and began its journey downstream. For the next hour, my thoughts followed it. At first, I imagined its life, starting as a tightly curled bud in spring, unfurling into a miniature solar panel, doing its work alongside thousands of others just like it. I wondered about the insects that might have scurried over its surface, the raindrops it had collected and shed, and the windstorms it had endured, clinging stubbornly to its branch. Now, here it was, alone for the first time, floating swiftly toward an unknown destination. Would it make it to the ocean, or would it snag on a tree root and decay into the riverbank? Would it sink quietly to the bottom, becoming part of the riverbed? My thoughts wandered with that leaf, meandering downstream, until eventually, it was time for me to move on. But even now, I remember that hour as one of the most peaceful and restorative I've ever spent. There was no agenda, no rush, just me, the river, and the quiet life of a single leaf.

Blending meditation and yoga with the forest is about letting go, tuning in, and finding a rhythm that feels real. The tree doesn't care if your downward dog is lopsided. The birds won't judge your breathing technique. What they *will* do is remind you: this moment is enough. And so are you.

Chapter Twelve

Eco-Consciousness

Spending time in the forest comes with a quiet responsibility. If we want to take the calm, the health benefits, the beauty, we must also give back, or at the very least, not take away anything more than we should.

True forest bathing means treading lightly, respecting the spaces that offer us so much.

More Than Just 'Leave No Trace'

Most people have heard the phrase *leave no trace*, and it's good advice. But eco-conscious forest bathing goes a step further. It asks us not only to avoid damaging nature, but to actively care for it, even if that means stepping a little outside our comfort zone.

It's easy to admire a view. It's another thing to shoulder a burden for it.

Years ago, during my guides training in Africa, we spent long days walking the bush on foot. Hours and hours, under the vast sky, learning to track, to notice, to respect the landscape we moved through. And every time we came across litter; an old water bottle, a rusty food tin, scraps of plastic, we were expected to pick it up, shove it in our rucksacks, and carry on. It didn't matter how hot it was, how heavy our bags already felt, or how filthy the rubbish was. It went into the bag.

Sometimes, by the end of the day, our packs were practically bursting with other people's rubbish. Sticky, smelly, unpleasant cargo we hadn't created but were responsible for nonetheless.

I'll be honest: there were moments I absolutely resented it.
Resented the thoughtlessness of the people who'd dropped it.
Resented the way it weighed down my pack.
Resented having to *deal* with it.

But somewhere along the line, that resentment shifted into something else. A kind of quiet determination. I realised that if I loved the land, really loved it, then caring for it wasn't something I could do only when it was easy or convenient.

It wasn't about feeling virtuous.
It wasn't about getting a pat on the back.
It was about doing what was needed, regardless of whether anyone noticed.

The Quiet Actions Matter

Forest bathing isn't a transaction: "I'll come here to relax, and in return,

I'll leave it as tidy as I found it."

It's a relationship.

It's choosing to be a good guest, even when no one is watching. Sometimes it's noticing a piece of litter tucked against a tree root and picking it up, even though you're not the one who left it. Sometimes it's stepping carefully around a patch of young seedlings rather than trampling through for a shortcut.

It's small acts of respect, repeated often enough that they become your default.

The Bigger Picture

On a wider scale, eco-conscious forest bathing means thinking about how our choices ripple outward. Supporting rewilding projects. Donating to forest conservation. Choosing local, sustainable products. Speaking up when green spaces are under threat.

Because if we truly want these places to be here for future generations, not just as backdrops for Instagram photos, but as living, breathing sanctuaries, we need to care for them now.

Not when it's easy.

Not when it's convenient.

Now.

And sometimes, yes, that means lugging around someone else's empty beer cans.

So what are the guidelines?

1. Leave No Trace

Yes, we've all *heard* it, but are we actually doing it?

- Stick to proper trails. Trampling through bluebells might make you feel like a fairy, but the crushed roots and compacted soil won't thank you.

- Take *all* your rubbish home. That includes "but it's natural" stuff like orange peel and sunflower seed shells. Foxes don't need your banana skins.

- Choose your sit spot with care, what looks like a peaceful clearing might be a nesting site, a frog hangout, or a rare orchid's last stand.

2. Forage Like a Forest Friend

Foraging is brilliant. It slows you down, gets you noticing what's edible, medicinal, or just plain magical. But if you're scooping up every elderflower in a ten-mile radius for your next gin experiment, you might want to rethink.

- Know what you're picking (and what you really shouldn't).

- Take a modest amount, enough for a recipe, not a business. Leave plenty for the bugs, birds, and other humans.

- If in doubt, just don't. Some places are legally or ecologically off-limits, and stealing a whole patch of wild garlic doesn't exactly help the woodland to thrive.

3. Give Something Back

You don't have to chain yourself to an oak tree to help. Conservation is full of small, do-able things that leave the land just a bit better off:

- Join or start a litter pick. It's oddly satisfying and low-key heroic.

- Plant a tree. Or ten. Or support people who do.

- Tackle invasive species if you know what you're doing. (Bracken-whacking can be surprisingly therapeutic.)

Because once you start paying attention to one patch of woodland, it becomes impossible not to wonder: Where else could this care take root?

4. Share the Good Word

The more people care, the more wild spaces stand a chance. Talking about your eco-habits can help, especially if you're not preachy about it.

- Lead by example. When you visit, leave the forest better than you found it. Maybe you tuck a piece of stray plastic into your pocket, or carefully move a branch off the path. These small, quiet actions speak volumes without needing a spotlight, often inspiring others simply by observation.

- Share what forest time *does* for you. The calm. The clarity. The small, good shifts in your mood. That stuff resonates more than stats.

- Big up local projects and charities doing the graft. If you can donate, great. If you can't, spreading the word still matters.

Caring for the forests starts with caring for how we show up in them. So if this book has helped you find that connection, sharing it with someone who might need it is another wonderful way to spread the good word.

Chapter Thirteen

Branching Out

Forest Bathing Around the World

From the lush, vibrant rainforests of Brazil to the misty, ancient woodlands of Ireland, people everywhere are rediscovering the power of nature therapy. What began as a Japanese practice has grown far beyond its roots, adapting to local landscapes and traditions while staying true to its core: the healing magic of the natural world.

Beyond the formal programmes, you only have to look at the **Nordic countries** to see a truly embedded approach to nature. For them, spending time outdoors is a way of life, even in the iciest months. Their relationship with the outdoors is built on both deep respect and a certain rugged enthusiasm, turning what many might see as a struggle into an everyday occurrence. Consider the Icelanders, for example, swimming outdoors all year round – many of them on a daily basis! Their public swimming baths are huge social hubs, used for catching up with friends and having a good old natter, much like our coffee shops here in Britain. Nordic winters, far from being a time to hibernate, are alive with outdoor traditions, stories, and folklore that truly embrace the cold and dark. This is a mindset instilled from an early age.

In **Sweden**, they call it "friluftsliv," or open-air living, a way of life that encourages a daily connection with nature. They've even got 'Ecotherapy in the Snow,' where guided winter walks are mixed with all sorts of snowy activities. It's real proof that staying active outdoors isn't just good for the body, it's a brilliant boost for the mind, too. Participants often leave feeling lighter, more awake, and a little less weighed down by life's daily grind.

Over in **Finland**, you'll find forest bathing meeting their famous sauna tradition. Picture a mix of icy air and then that deep, penetrating warmth. The contrast is something else – it just jolts the senses awake, making the world feel sharper, clearer, and infinitely less mundane.

And up in the far north of **Norway**, where daylight becomes just a distant memory in winter, forest bathing takes on a truly dreamlike quality. Lantern-lit walks under the northern lights, turn what could be oppressive darkness into something almost otherworldly.

In **Scotland**, for instance, they're so convinced of nature's power that doctors are actually prescribing woodland walks! Programmes like

'**Branching Out**' run for twelve weeks, with folk spending three hours each week getting stuck into all sorts. It's not just gentle walks either. We're talking outdoor tai chi, getting your hands properly mucky with rhododendron clearance, learning bushcraft like fire lighting, or tapping into your inner artist with willow sculptures. They even get proper certificates at the end – a 'tool handling certificate' no less, and a John Muir Discovery Award! The whole idea is to help people feel more confident, boost their mental health, and build a real sense of community, all amongst the trees.

Not to be outdone, **South Korea**, seeing the good work happening in Japan, has also truly embraced forest healing. They've gone all in, setting up dedicated 'forest healing centres' in their beautiful forested regions, aiming to provide those same mental health and wellness benefits for their own citizens. It's fantastic to see such a dedicated approach spreading across the globe.

Over in the **United States**, while perhaps not yet as ingrained in everyday life as in some places, forest therapy programmes are definitely gaining ground. Organisations like the **Association of Nature and Forest Therapy (ANFT)** are doing brilliant work, training up guides all over the place. It's quite incredible actually, they've trained people in over sixty countries, creating a truly global network of forest therapy guides. This helps ensure that wherever you are, there's likely someone nearby who can help you connect with nature and experience its healing.

Local Terms, Same Idea

The language of forest bathing may differ, but the heart of it remains the same. In the United States, people talk about "nature therapy," while in Australia, it's "bush therapy," inspired by the continent's wild and rugged landscapes. No matter the name, the goal is shared: to reconnect with the earth and let its steadying presence work its magic.

Joining Forces

International collaborations are helping to deepen our understanding of forest bathing. Researchers and organisations are pooling their knowledge, holding conferences, and sharing techniques. **The International Nature and Forest Therapy Alliance,** for example, brings together practitioners from across the globe to exchange ideas and grow this movement. These efforts remind us that caring for nature and ourselves is a shared responsibility.

As forest bathing grows beyond its Japanese roots, it's clear that this isn't just a passing trend. It's a testament to our deep-seated need to be part of the natural world. Whether you're strolling through a local park or exploring a remote forest, you're part of a global movement that's bringing people closer to the earth, and to each other.

But as this movement spreads its wings, it also opens up an incredible opportunity. It's a chance to really listen, to truly learn from cultures and traditions that have always held nature close, with a bond so deep it's practically woven into their fabric. That's where we're heading next; exploring those ancient insights that can truly change how we see our place in the wild.

Chapter Fourteen

Cultural Insights

We've just seen how forest bathing is finding its feet all over the world, adapting and growing in so many different places. But beyond the workshops and the health policies, there's a much deeper well of wisdom to draw from.

For centuries, across every continent, people have understood that nature is our teacher, our healer, and our kin. In this chapter, we're going to dive into some of those profound cultural insights, particularly from Indigenous communities, who have always known what it means to truly live with the land, not just on it. It's about listening, learning, and letting their ancient wisdom guide us towards an even richer relationship with the wild.

Learning from Indigenous People and Cultures

From the towering trees to the sweeping deserts and the rugged mountain ranges, Indigenous peoples have lived in ways that show us how to truly listen to the land. Their traditions offer wisdom that's not only accurate and proven but also incredibly relevant to today's forest bathers.

They teach us the importance of sustainable living, showing how to use resources without depleting them and preserving ecosystems for future generations. We can learn from their practices of mindful harvesting, which ensures that plants and animals are not overexploited. Their deep understanding of medicinal plants and natural remedies provides valuable insights into holistic health and well-being.

Spiritual Connection and Reciprocity

Indigenous communities also emphasize the spiritual connection to the land, treating it with reverence and gratitude. The Native American practice of thanking a tree before it's felled, or the Aboriginal commitment to "Caring for Country," isn't just poetic sentiment, it's a way of living that sees every stream, stone, and breeze as part of a shared life. Beyond gratitude, many Native American traditions truly embody the principle of **reciprocity** – the understanding that life is a constant exchange. When nature provides for us, whether it's a berry bush or a flowing river, we in turn have a responsibility to give back, to care for the land, and to ensure its well-being for future generations. By listening to and learning from Indigenous wisdom, we can gain a greater appreciation for the natural world before it's too late.

African Wisdom: The Trackers' Way

Moving to another continent, the wisdom of the **San Bushmen** in Southern Africa offers a truly astonishing lesson in connection. Their tracking skills are legendary, but it's far more than just following footprints. To truly track an animal, a San tracker practically *becomes* the animal. They imagine themselves in its skin, thinking like it, moving like it, understanding why it would turn left or right, or stop to browse. They develop an uncanny ability to detect subtle scents that most of us lost generations ago. It's an almost magical attunement, a truly awesome example of observing the land with every single one of your senses, not just your eyes.

The Sky as a Compass: Polynesian Wisdom

Sometimes, observing the land means looking up, way up, to the night sky. For the **Polynesian voyagers**, the stars, moon, sun, and even the currents and winds were their living, breathing map. Their incredible skill in celestial navigation, known as **'Wayfinding,'** allowed them to travel vast oceans without instruments, guided purely by their intimate, intuitive knowledge of the cosmos and the ocean. It was a profound connection, a deep trust in natural cues that meant the sky truly was their compass. Their wisdom teaches us that knowing the stars is a way to deepen our sensory awareness and feel deeply connected to the larger rhythms of the planet, even when we're just gazing up from our local woodland, (pondering the frequency that Sirius hums at!).

Treading Carefully

Learning from Indigenous practices comes with responsibilities. It's one thing to be inspired by these traditions, but it's another to claim them or strip them of their meaning. Respect is essential, and a little humility goes a long way.

- **Do your homework.** Learn about the Indigenous communities in your area and their relationships with the land.

- **Give credit where it's due.** When sharing your experiences, acknowledge the origins of the practices that have guided you.

Building Bridges

The best lessons often come from meaningful exchanges. Many Indigenous leaders and communities are open to sharing their wisdom with those who approach with genuine curiosity and respect. Here's a snapshot from my travel blog, capturing a day etched in my memory from a trip to the rainforests of Australia some years ago now:

Day 216 – Sunday, 6th December 2009 – Tjapukai and Bama Bulurra

What an absolutely amazing day. It began early with a stock-up mission for snot rags and flu remedies, less glamorous but essential, before we made our way to the Aboriginal Park. There, we spent the morning with the Tjabba-ghand-ji clan, diving into their shocking and very recent history, their beliefs, and their customs. (I still can't fathom how it was legal to shoot an Aboriginal person during the first ten years of my life.)

Through dances, songs, and traditional fire-starting demonstrations, they shared their world with us. Then, we headed out onto their land, where they taught us how to throw spears and boomerangs, play the didgeridoo, and forage in the rainforest; a crash course in survival and respect.

With a fantastic packed lunch in hand, we climbed back into Betsy (our trusty but temperamental campervan) and drove an hour north to meet the Walker brothers, members of a neighbouring tribe. The directions were brilliantly simple: follow the coast road past Port Douglas, turn right towards Cooya Beach, and drive until you reach "the most massive tree at the end." They'd be waiting.

Sure enough, we found the massive tree. The brothers? Not so much. What we did find, though, was a sign warning us about saltwater crocodiles and sternly advising against going near the water. Little did we know, a couple of hours later, we'd be wading into that same water, spear in hand, hunting for mud crabs.

Linc Walker soon arrived and led us on an extraordinary walk through the beach forest. He pointed out medicinal plants, tools, and creatures that had supported his family for generations. We were spellbound as he explained how every inch of this land was home and provider. Then, he invited us to his house, where fresh mangoes and gold-

en syrup-slathered bread waited alongside his incredible collection of artifacts: burnie-beans, turtle shells, swordfish teeth, and whale bones.

Fueled up and armed with spears, we followed Linc into the mangrove swamps, just metres from those crocodile warnings. Along the way, we sampled green ants (excellent for flu and tasting like intense lemon), hibiscus leaves, beach almonds, and a curious plum-apricot hybrid from the shoreline. Inside the swamps, the heat was suffocating, and the mosquitoes were relentless, so we retreated to the shallows of the sea, prodding the sand ahead of us to avoid stingrays. (Stingrays!? I mean, wasn't Steve Irwin...? Never mind, I stabbed at that sand like my life depended on it.)

Despite our efforts, the day's haul was modest: one mud crab, a few giant winkles, some mud skippers, and cone snails. Back at Linc's, my back now a buffet of mosquito bites, he brought out a jar of dugong fat to ease the itching. (Later, we looked it up. Dugongs are like a cross between a whale and a manatee. Who knew?)

Hot, mosquito-bitten, educated, and reeking of whale fat, we drove back to Cairns along the coast road, awestruck by the depth and beauty of the Aboriginal way of life. That evening, we prepared for another immersion into Tjapukai culture, but the lessons of the day stayed with me, a reminder that nature is not just a resource but a relationship, one built on respect, reciprocity, and reverence.

The experience was a sharp reminder that there's always more to learn if we're willing to listen. Whether it's sharing a meal, hearing stories, or walking through the forest with those who know it best, it's not just about picking up knowledge, it's about seeing our place in the natural world with fresh eyes.

So if you ever get the chance, whether it's in the wilds of an exotic rainforest or just in your local area;

- **Attend workshops or talks led by local guides.** These guides offer a mix of survival skills, cultural tales, and a magical way of looking at nature that makes every leaf and pebble feel like it's part of a grand cosmic plan. Plus, you get to learn how to approach nature with a sense of gratitude and care that's often missing in our fast-paced lives.

- **Support Indigenous-led conservation efforts.** Support is vital for preserving biodiversity and cultural heritage. Indigenous communities have lived in harmony with their environments for generations, offering unique insights into sustainable practices. By supporting their leadership in conservation, we not only protect precious ecosystems but also honor and empower these original stewards of the land. This collaborative approach ensures that conservation efforts are holistic, respectful, and deeply connected to the land's history and future.

- **Engage in thoughtful dialogue with Indigenous communities.** Conversations can reveal how traditional practices and perspectives align with forest bathing, showing us ways to incorporate these insights without appropriating or diminishing their cultural significance. For instance, rather than simply borrowing rituals or symbols, we can explore the underlying principles. Ask ourselves how these values can guide our time in the forest? What can we learn about living in harmony with the natural world?

By staying curious and keeping our egos in check, we get the chance to see why these traditions have lasted for generations, and how they can still teach us a thing or two about respect.

International Forest Therapy Events

In the heart of Finland's wooded landscapes, a unique annual event unfolds, drawing together a diverse group of individuals united by a single passion: the healing power of nature. The International Forest Therapy Day has rapidly evolved from a modest gathering into a significant event on the global stage of forest therapy. The conference typically features workshops, guided forest walks, and sessions led by experts in the field of forest therapy. Participants have the opportunity to learn about the latest research, share experiences, and connect with others who are interested in promoting the connection between forests and human well-being.

Then there is **The International Congress ISFT.** A prestigious scientific event initiated by the International Society of Forest Therapy. This annual congress rotates locations each year, taking place in various countries around the world. It attracts experts, scientists, researchers, and practitioners dedicated to exploring the vital connections between forest ecosystems and human health.

The congress is a platform for presenting cutting-edge research, sharing best practices, and showcasing case studies of the non-wood forest economy and forest therapies in public health and nature-based tourism. Participants have the opportunity to attend workshops, keynote speeches, and interactive panel discussions led by world-renowned experts in therapeutic forest tourism and public health.

This event aims to advance our understanding of how forest ecosystem services can enhance human and environmental health, and it provides a great opportunity for networking, collaboration, and learning from the world's leading experts.

So, we've had a bit of a wander through some incredible cultural insights. It's clear as day that what we call 'forest bathing' is just one way humans have connected with nature across a huge, ancient stretch of time. By leaning into the wisdom of Indigenous folks, and soaking up the shared knowledge from these big global get-togethers, we can help grow this whole exciting movement.

It really hammers home that it's not just about finding a bit of peace for ourselves. It's about truly grasping that deep, real relationship between us and the living world – the one so many cultures have instinctively cherished for thousands of years. It reminds you there's always another layer to discover, a new feeling to unearth, and more respect to offer when you step into the wild. And honestly, I can't think of anything more brilliant than that.

CHAPTER FIFTEEN

Community

The Warmth of the Group

A Christian friend once explained why she never misses church on a Sunday. She said it was like being a lump of coal in a fire. Take the coal out, and it quickly cools, losing its heat and light. But nestle it back in with the others, and it glows again, warm, bright, and alive.

I remember nodding politely at the time, but the concept stuck with me. Maybe because it's just as true for our connection with the natural world. Drift away from it, and something essential starts to dim. There's even a name for it now: **Nature Deficit Disorder**. Sounds like something you'd need a prescription for, but it's really just what happens when you've been indoors too long with nothing but screens for company.

The thing about forest bathing is, when you do it with others, it's like stepping back into the fire. You don't just warm yourself, you can light each other up as well.

Starting a Forest Bathing Group

Starting a group might sound like a big deal, but really, it's just like planting a seed. No spreadsheets or six-point plans needed. Just a bit of care, a pinch of patience, and the willingness to give it a go.

Here's how to begin, gently of course.

1. Find Your People

Who do you picture standing quietly in the woods beside you? A friend who needs a break? A neighbour you only wave at but always mean to talk to? Someone you know who could do with a bit of grounding? Invite people who are open to slowing down, even if they're not the "outdoorsy" type.

2. Know Your Why

What's the reason behind it? To explore new trails, make space for calm, or share the restorative power of the woods? Knowing your *why* will help shape the group, and it comes in handy when you're trying to explain it to someone who thinks it all sounds a bit odd.

3. Pick Your Channels

You don't need a logo or a launch date. Just a way to stay in touch. A WhatsApp group works well. Facebook if you're reaching further. Or plain old email if that's more your style. It doesn't have to be perfect, it just has to be easy and useful.

4. Plan Your First Gathering

Keep it simple. A local park, a patch of woodland, or even a tree-lined footpath will do. The point isn't how far you go, it's how present you are. Encourage everyone to dress for the weather, bring water, and silence their phones (or better yet, leave them behind!).

5. Let it Settle

If the first session feels awkward, that's completely normal. Once people relax into it, a quiet rhythm starts to form, and that's when the good stuff happens.

How to Keep Things Sane

Getting people together is one thing. Keeping the mood right is another. Here are a few soft rules that help with group dynamics:

- **Respect the different speeds.** Some people want to pause every few steps. Others want to keep moving. Let both exist.

- **Cater to curiosities.** Birdwatchers, tree geeks, silence-seekers, bring in little moments that appeal to all kinds.

- **Welcome the quiet.** Remind everyone that silence isn't awkward here. It's part of the point.

Things to Try as a Group

Want to add a little something to the experience? Here are a few gentle, low-key additions that tend to work well.

- **Guided meditation.** A few minutes of stillness at the start or end. Nothing grand, just noticing the air, the smells, the sound of leaves, all the things we've talked about so far.

- **Sensory walks.** Spend a few minutes focusing on just one sense at a time. What do you hear? What do you smell? It slows everyone down beautifully.

- **Nature art.** Bring sketchbooks, crayons, or just your eyes. Afterwards, share what stood out. You'll be amazed what others saw that you missed.

The Power of Sharing

When I guide safari groups in Zambia, we always finish with the same question: *What was the best thing about today?* Lions or birds, sunsets or silence; it's never the same, and that's the beauty of it.

You can use the same idea at the end of your walks.

- **Reflection circle.** Invite people to share one thing they noticed or felt. Doesn't have to be deep, just a moment that stood out.

- **Photo sharing.** Set up a shared album if people take pictures. It builds connection between walks.

- **Gratitude moments.** Before everyone heads off, go round the group and each name one thing they're thankful for. It ends things on a lovely note.

Forest bathing with others is about being human, connected in nature. Seeing how differently we all experience the same place. So whether it's someone you know well, or someone you haven't met yet, extend the invite. Pull them into the green spaces with you.

The trees are already waiting, and the fire always burns warmer when we're in it together.

Community Gardens & Allotments

In the middle of our concrete sprawl, community gardens thankfully pop up like determined dandelions in a pavement crack these days. Yes, they're about plants, but they're also about people. About finding a patch of calm in the honking, beeping mess of city life. About growing things you can actually eat and maybe, if you're lucky, growing a bit of community spirit along the way.

I didn't really get this until my mum took on an allotment right in the centre of town. I wasn't expecting much, some cracked paving slabs, a few tatty cabbages, and a shed clinging on with rust and optimism. But when I walked through those gates? Whole other world. Trees, birds, rows of bean poles standing to attention, it was like Narnia, but with fewer lions and more compost. I actually forgot I was still in town. There were neighbours swapping tools and stories, making each other tea, swapping tips over the best way to deal with aphids. It was community, in wellies.

The Little Oasis with Big Impact

The magic of a community garden is that once you're inside, the city sort of fades out. Between the courgettes and the crocosmia, something lovely happens; you focus. You notice things again. That's forest bathing, city-style. No need to disappear into a wilderness just get your hands in the soil and notice the bees.

When I visit Mum's allotment, it's not the veggies that impress me most, it's how every job, however small, slows you down. Watering, weeding, just pottering really. You start noticing what the soil needs. You notice what *you* need. Suddenly you're not thinking about emails or bin day. You're just present.

In a community garden, you can forest bathe with a cuppa in hand. In a safe space. You can pay attention to the way dew hangs on a kale leaf, or the quiet bustle of bees going about their bee business.

So You Fancy Starting One?

It sounds big, but honestly, it starts small. Someone once looked at Mum's allotment, a forgotten scrap of land with more nettles than promise, and thought, "We could do something here." And they did.

Look around your area. Vacant lot? Scruffy verge? Sad bit of park no one visits? Potential. Rooftops, old car parks, the scraggly edges of football fields are all fair game. You don't need permission from the King, just a bit of enthusiasm and someone willing to ask the council if it's alright.

Rallying the Troops

When we started caring for our little patch of woodland in Sussex, I thought it might be a two-person job involving me, him, and a pair of loppers. Turns out, people were *desperate* to get involved. One Facebook post and a few biscuit-bribed conversations later, we had a Sunday crew. Some came to help, others came for the photos, and a few just came to stand around and breathe. And that's fine too.

Start small. Organise a chat, a walk, a nosy round a possible site. People like to feel included, not recruited.

Keeping the Wheels Turning

Mum's allotment has a committee, I guess a bit like a village WI but with more mud. One plans the plots, one organises workdays, someone else brings the biscuits. (Essential role. Never undervalue the Biscuit Person.)

It doesn't need to be fancy. Just a few folks who care and aren't afraid to remind each other when it's time to strim the paths or send out a group text. With everyone bringing their own quirks and skills, the garden ends up feeling properly alive, not just with runner beans, but with personality.

Mindful Gardening (Without Having to Call It That)

A London friend once told me her allotment was the first place time slowed down for her. I thought she was being poetic until I visited. Expected to find her battling bindweed, instead found her sitting cross-legged, watching a bee bumble its way through the marigolds.

She looked like a monk in fleece. Totally still. I nearly backed away in case I broke the spell.

When she finally spoke, she just said, "Do you hear that?"
I didn't, at first. Then I did. The birdsong. Distant laughter. A wheelbarrow squeaking somewhere. It wasn't silent, it was *full* of sound. But it was the kind of sound you don't notice until you stop doing the hundred other things you're usually doing.

She told me the garden taught her how to *notice* again. How to be where her feet were. And now, I get it.

There's something grounding about being up to your elbows in soil. Planting a seed with no guarantee it'll come good, but doing it anyway. Watching something grow because you *waited*, not because you forced it.

Gardens are slow. They don't rush. And in a world that never shuts up, that's a pretty powerful thing.

You come for the veg. You stay for the headspace. And maybe the jam swaps.

So what more could you want from a patch of land?

Fresh mint, quiet moments, someone to lend you a spade, and maybe a few unexpected friendships. That's a good return, I'd say.

Volunteering for Green Spaces: Giving Back Through Nature

When I think about the spaces that have cradled me through life's ups and downs, the forests I've wandered to clear my mind or the parks where I've found stillness, I'm struck by how much I owe to these places. They've been my escape, my solace, my grounding. And when I walk through them, it's easy to forget they don't just stay beautiful on their own. They need us as much as we need them.

Take Mum's new allotment, for instance. When she first got the plot, it was a mess of overgrown brambles, tough old couch grass and forgotten weeds running wild. It would have been easy to dismiss it as a hopeless tangle, but with patience and persistence, she transformed it. Now, it's a lush little haven buzzing with life, where neighbours chat over steaming mugs of tea, trade seeds, and help each other lug heavy bags of compost. She is building connection and strengthening community, all whilst boosting her immune system.

Conservation Volunteering

Volunteering for conservation is about getting your hands dirty in the best way possible. It might mean planting trees, clearing invasive species, or fixing up public footpaths, but it's not just a free gym, it's deeply rewarding, ask any gardener. You're actively giving back to the spaces that give so much to you.

When we started rewilding our woodland all those years ago, I wasn't prepared for how much it would change me. There's something about chopping through rhodies or hacking new access paths with others that brings you back to the present moment. As well as clearing a way, we were creating connections, with the land, with each other, and with ourselves. It made me notice the small things more: the silver weed battling the meadow grasses along the woodland verges, or the way the sound travels oddly over the undulations of the land.

And then there's the pride of making real progress: standing back and admiring a patch of ground where bracken once dominated, now clear. Or the absolute joy when those bluebell seeds we painstakingly spread begin to carpet ground that was once choked by evergreen rhododendron. With cleared spaces come new life, too – wildflowers popping up where they hadn't before, and the flutter of new butterflies or moths drawn to the revived habitat. It wasn't all perfectly planned success either! There were plenty of laughs (and lots of mud) during trial and error bushcraft projects, like the clay oven we built a bit too large, or the dam that was perhaps a tad too small to hold back the autumn downpours. But every experiment was a lesson, leading to new skills learned, and crucially, improving our range of edible campfire recipes!

And that's the beauty of conservation volunteering: it works both ways. While you're helping nature, it's quietly working on you, showing you things you'd otherwise miss in the rush of daily life – all the while pumping you full of fresh air and feel-good chemicals. What's not to like!?

The Joy of Giving Back

I once joined a group of volunteers clearing an area of rampant overgrown bracken from a public woodland. As we hacked back the chest-high greenery and thick brambles, someone uncovered a long-forgotten bench. I'll never forget the cheer that went up, something so simple, yet so satisfying. By the end of the day, families were walking through that space again, stopping to rest on that bench as if it had always been there. Seeing the immediate impact of your efforts is such a rare and beautiful thing in this world of instant everything.

Another time, I helped a friend plant a wildflower meadow in a neglected corner at the end of her cul-de-sac. At first, it looked like nothing more than a stony dirt patch, but over the months, it transformed into a vibrant sea of colour. Seeing bees, butterflies, and even children chasing each other through the flowers brought such a sense of pride. It was so much more than a meadow... it was a living, breathing reminder of what a little effort and patience could achieve.

Then there was the time I joined a community beach clean-up. It was a cold, blustery day, the kind where you question why you ever got persuaded to leave the house, but by the end of it, we had collected mountains of rubbish. Plastic bottles, old fishing nets, and even a rusted shopping trolley, things that had no place in the natural beauty of the coastline. As the sun broke through the clouds, we stood back and looked at the clean stretch we'd revealed. Watching flocks of birds land on the now-pristine shore made every freezing gust of wind worthwhile.

Sometimes, it's the simplest acts, clearing a path, planting seeds, or picking up litter, that make the biggest difference to both the land and the people who share it.

What Can You Do?

If you're curious about how you can help, start small. Find a local conservation group or ask your nearest park if they need volunteers. It might be a couple of hours pulling weeds or a weekend planting trees, but every bit counts.

The point is, you don't need to be an expert or commit endless hours. Just show up with a pair of gloves and a willingness to help. And before long, you might find yourself growing something more than plants; you'll grow presence, connection, and an appreciation for the spaces that keep us all grounded.

Beyond hands-on work, another powerful way to build community and encourage connection with nature in the modern world is through sharing your experiences online.

The Magic of Social Media: Sharing the Joy of Forest Bathing

Mental health challenges are on the rise, so encouraging others to step outside and connect with nature has never been more crucial. By sharing your own experiences, you could make a real difference in someone else's life.

A simple post about how forest bathing has helped you feel calmer, more focused, or less stressed might reach someone who really needs it. Authentic and personal stories resonate more deeply, so talk about how being in the forest made you feel, whether it helped clear your mind or melt away the stress of a long week. Those small moments can inspire someone to take their first step into the woods.

Practical tips like tuning into the sounds, sights, or smells of nature can be incredibly helpful for newcomers. Hashtags like #ForestBathing or #NatureHealing make it easy to connect with others who share your passion. A single timely post could remind someone miles away to take a break and get outside for a woodland walk.

If you're feeling inspired, you could even create an online group or page to bring people together. Share tips on great spots to visit, mindful walk ideas, or snippets about why you love forest bathing. You'll quickly build a community of like-minded individuals encouraging each other to spend more time in nature.

Protect What You Love

One thing to keep in mind when posting is how to keep those special spots special. Instead of tagging exact locations, try focusing on the vibe or the experience. Overcrowding can take away some of the magic and even harm the environment, so it's always good to think about what's best for the space. Sharing reminders like sticking to public footpaths, taking out what you take in, and respecting the wildlife can also help make sure these places stay beautiful for generations to come.

Speaking from experience as a safari guide, I always remind my guests to check that geo-tagging is switched off on their devices. There was one particular instance that really drove this point home. A guest had shared some incredible photos of a rhino we had spotted, but they didn't realize that their phone camera's location tagging was on. Thankfully, we caught it before it went online, but it was a stark reminder of how easy it is to inadvertently give away the whereabouts of endangered species. In regions where poaching is a serious threat, something as simple as an innocent photo share could have devastating consequences.

By being mindful and turning off geo-tagging, we can enjoy and share our experiences without compromising the safety of these magnificent creatures. It's a small step that makes a big difference. So next time you're out there, whether it's in the forest or on safari, double-check those settings and help protect the spaces and wildlife we cherish. In the UK, this is particularly important for rare bird nest sites and protected species.

But what about those times when getting out isn't an option? Perhaps the weather is against us, time is tight, or big adventures simply aren't on the cards. Thankfully, the healing power of nature isn't confined to the outdoors. Even within the comfort of our own homes, we can create a sanctuary that continues to nurture our well-being...

CHAPTER SIXTEEN

Bringing Nature Indoors

Greening My Inner Space

I love coming home to my little house in Sussex. When I open my front door and step inside, I'm greeted by a calm, leafy haven. Some might call it a small jungle, (one that doesn't bite and mostly behaves, as long as I remember to water it occasionally). But for me, houseplants are so much more than just a trendy home accessory or something I awkwardly apologise to when they start looking crispy. They are part of my family, and have been for over three decades.

Why I Bother With Indoor Plants

Sure, they look nice, but these leafy mates are doing far more than just sprucing up my shelves. They're quietly purifying the air, boosting my mood, and generally making my home smell less like last nights dinner and feel more like a natural cosy woodland glade (minus the mud).

Plants are brilliant at hoovering up all sorts of airborne nasties; chemicals like formaldehyde and benzene that sneak in via carpets, paint, and cleaning products. They also pump out oxygen, help regulate humidity, and can even cut down on breathable bacteria and mould spores.

And it seems I'm not the only one catching on to this magic. The indoor plant market was worth nearly 20 billion dollars in 2023 and is expected to climb well past 28 billion by 2031. That's a hell of a lot of plant pets!

Which Plants I Choose

If you're thinking of adding some potted relatives to your home, I suggest starting with the easy ones. The ones that won't throw a hissy fit if you forget to water them now and then. From my experience, plants like spider plants (you know, those familiar spiky pale green ones with little 'babies' that dangle?), snake plants, and simple ivy are those forgiving types who'll soldier on through your busy week and poke up with occasional neglect.

I love adding a splash of colour with something flowering, or if I want drama without the maintenance, succulents rarely disappoint. I've even found some plants that moonlight as dehumidifiers, which is handy if your bathroom tends to feel like a tropical rainforest or you have poor circulation in any rooms. Ferns, English ivy, and peace lilies are particularly good at relentlessly sucking moisture from the air.

Planting Without the Plot

You certainly don't need to live in a botanical garden or build an indoor greenhouse to start. A windowsill jungle, a vertical wall of herbs, or a cluster of pots on a shelf all count. I'm a big fan of using what you've got: old mugs, chipped teapots, that weird ornamental container you've never had a use for.

Hanging planters, terrariums, plant stands made from milk crates – if it can hold soil and a little hope, I say it's fair game.

How I Try Not To Kill Them

The trick I've learned is to figure out where your plant comes from and to recreate their natural habitat (on a budget, in your lounge, of course!).

For my succulents? They like it dry, sunny, and not too clingy. My orchids? They want rainforest vibes; humid, dappled light, and no cold drafts. My spider plants? They'd rather be somewhere warm and steamy, like my kitchen near the kettle, and that's because they are native to the undergrowth of forested areas, mountainous regions, or along riversides and bushes in tropical and Southern Africa. You'd typically find them thriving in warm temperatures between 18-32°C (65-90°F) and they're actually quite drought-tolerant thanks to their thick, fleshy roots that store water, which is probably why they're so forgiving indoors!

My latest challenge is carnivorous plants. I need them to chow down on any stray biting insects that venture into my space. I've tried a few times in the past with limited success; those hanging pitchers simply didn't grow big enough to attract or catch anything. I'd absolutely love to try the UK native Sundew, but I'm a bit nervous about providing enough "food" for them – and, dare I say it, the risk of attracting even more flies through any open windows! But it's a challenge I'm keen to tackle again.

At my place, things have got a bit out of hand. I've had some of my houseplants for over 20 years. They've had children. Some of those have had their own children. It's practically a green family reunion in every room. I've taken in neglected stragglers from friends' houses and even staged a rescue mission when I saw a once-beautiful plant languishing on someone's windowsill, slowly turning to toast. I brought it home like an abandoned kitten. Thankfully it's thriving now.

Caring for them has become a treasured part of my day. I check them over, deadheading, watering, encouraging them to climb or trail in the direction that avoids my furniture. And in return, they help me breathe easier, calm my mind, and generally stop me from ever having to worry about moldy cupboards. Not bad for something that lives in a terracotta pot.

Biophilic Design

As we touched on earlier, "Biophilia" is a fancy term for something most of us already know deep down: we like being around nature because it makes us feel better. For me, biophilic design is just the act of bringing that outside-goodness inside, in thoughtful and aesthetic ways.

I try to incorporate elements where I can:

- **See it** – swapping out a picture frame for a living wall, or just sticking a fern in the loo.

- **Hear and smell it** – gentle water features, wooden textures, a dab of essential oil that smells like a pine forest.

- **Feel it** – natural materials under my feet, smooth pebbles on a table, warm clay mugs in my hands.

- **Be reminded of it** – creating indoor nooks that feel like forest clearings. A comfy chair surrounded by green things. Places where I can see the bird feeder outside the window and watch the rain running off the leaves.

Making Your Indoor Garden Yours

Ultimately, it's your house, your jungle rules. Whether you fancy a few herbs on the kitchen counter, a DIY hydroponic lettuce farm, or a full-blown vertical wall of ivy and trailing vines, go for it. Even just a jam jar of mint on the windowsill can be the beginning of something lovely (and it smells amazing every time you brush past it).

My Takeaway

My main takeaway is this: you don't have to be green-fingered or a full-time plant whisperer. Just bring a few leafy companions into your space and see how it feels.

I've found it's not about being perfect or keeping every pot pristine; it's about reconnecting with life in all its quiet, oxygen-puffing, leaf-unfurling glory.

When you make space for green things to live alongside you, you notice more. A new shoot. An emerging flower. That ridiculous way my peace lily flops over like a teenager when it's thirsty. It's an activity that forces us to slow down, pay attention, and maybe even start keeping track of the small things. Which brings me to one of my favourite practices: nature journaling.

CHAPTER SEVENTEEN

Nature Journaling

The Case for a Nature Journal

I've kept a journal, in one form or another, since I was a little girl. It started with a very small spiral-bound notebook and the pride of sketching a half-decent, recognisable skylark I'd copied from a bird book. That tiny drawing encouraged me to do more, and ever since, my journal has been the most valuable companion through every season of my life.

Your notebook or nature journal is not a diary. It's not homework. Think of it more like a catch-all for the things that make you stop and go "wow" (or even just "huh?"). A place for sketches, leaf rubbings, odd thoughts, questions, poems, weather notes, feelings, fungi sightings, or whatever else your wandering self wants to record.

No one is going to mark it, but the marks you make will be magic.

Choosing Your Companion

You don't need a special notebook, but having one you like definitely helps. Something that can survive the odd splash or muddy rucksack. Something that feels good in your hands. Maybe with paper thick enough for the occasional watercolour blob, or slim enough to tuck in your coat pocket. Imitation leather? Recycled spiral pad? Doesn't matter. If it makes you want to write or draw, it's the right one.

There Are No Rules

Don't get precious or try to impress anyone. You're not submitting it for review. It's just you and the outside world having a bit of a chat. You might include:

- **Observations** – the robin that stared you down, the way frost edges the leaves, your neighbour's hedge exploding into blossom overnight.

- **Reflections** – what that felt like, what it reminded you of, why it mattered that day.

- **Sketches or Paintings** – even quick scribbles have power. You're not aiming for gallery-ready. You're aiming for captured.

- **Found Things** – pressed petals, rubbings of bark, a fallen feather. (Nature provides these gifts, but if it's alive or housing something, leave it be.)

Why Bother?

Because it slows you down, in a good way. It gets you to look, not just glance. And in doing that, it brings you back to the present. Here's why you might find yourself reaching for your journal again and again:

- **You notice more, profoundly.** There's a lime tree on my local walk that I often stop at to check a woodpecker nest hole. One day, as I was looking up, a pair of joined leaves fell directly onto my hand. As I studied them, I saw they looked like lungs, and noticed the veins went all the way to the edges. Suddenly, the message was clear: I should breathe deeply, all the way to the edges of my lungs. That's the kind of unexpected connection that only happens when you slow down and truly look, ready to capture it.

- **It helps you feel and learn without trying.** Sometimes, when I'm out walking in the woods, I "receive" a word – or maybe the word is already swirling in my head, I'm never quite sure. It might be something like **Pride** or **Hope**, a word I sense I need to get to know better. I then look around for signs of that word in nature: a tree standing proud, or a tiny sapling hopefully battling high winds. My journal becomes a space to explore that word further, perhaps researching it in different languages, its origins or root words, then maybe doodling it using different styles and fonts. I find doodling a form of meditation, one word invariably leads on to another and another. Before I know it, an hour of "meditation" has passed and I feel calm and ready to tackle my to-do list.

- **It anchors you, no matter what.** Some days are busy or bleak. The world feels too much, too loud. At those times, I simply flip back to the beginning of my journal and peruse each page. By the time I have reviewed the whole thing, I am usually smiling or feeling much better. The reminders throughout are like a trip down memory lane, and I relive those walks, those moments of quiet connection. It's proof I was present. Proof I noticed something real.

Getting Started

You don't need a plan. Just take your journal and a pencil next time you head out. Sit on a bench. Linger by a tree. Stand in your garden with your morning cuppa. Write something down. That's it.

Some people make a daily habit of it. Others only open the thing once a season. Doesn't matter. What matters is that it's yours, and that it reminds you, when the world gets loud again, how to listen. And that gentle art of listening, of weaving nature into even the busiest days, is exactly what we'll explore next, as we look at how small, regular doses of green can transform your daily routine.

CHAPTER EIGHTEEN

Daily Routines

Making Tree Time Part of Your Life

The practice of nature connection isn't reserved for weekends or wild places, it's something that can be folded into daily life without too much effort. A moment at the window, a breath of fresh air on the walk to the shops. The sound of birdsong while the kettle boils.

Our to-do lists are already full and finding time seems impossible, so this chapter is more about shifting the way you use your time to focus on what's around you and bring a small piece of green into each day.

The key here is to be consistent, to make it a new habit. I once read somewhere that if you do something for 30 days in a row it becomes a habit – so that's what you're aiming for. (I've tried testing this theory a number of times by brushing my teeth in chair pose, but have yet to make it to 30 days, so I can't say if it works or not!)

One foot in the world, one foot on the earth

We all have routines. The commute. The lunch break. The post-dinner scroll. It's easy for these parts of the day to blur past unnoticed. But what if one of them became a standing date with a tree, a stretch of sky, or a quiet patch of grass? You don't need a whole hour. Two or three minutes of presence, real presence, can shift your state more than half an hour of distracted scrolling ever could.

Ideas:

- Step outside before checking your phone in the morning. Breathe to the very edges of your lungs a few times.

- **Commute:** Noticing clouds, trees, or even just the sky from a bus or train window. Walk or cycle part of your journey instead of driving.

- **Workday:** Looking out a window at a tree, keeping a plant on the desk, or taking a minute to step outside for a specific sensory observation (e.g., listening for birds during a break, or finding a new patch of green).

- **Evenings:** A brief moment of stargazing before bed, or listening to the sounds of the night. Watch the moon each night for a week and notice how it changes.

Building a habit without making it a chore

The goal isn't perfection. It's not about ticking boxes. It's about making nature feel like a normal part of your day, not something you have to "go do," but something you fall into naturally, like a favourite jumper.

The more these moments happen, the easier they become. You start to notice the birdsong before the traffic. You pause under the same tree each day. You catch yourself smiling at the precise and impressive flight path of a hoverfly. That's when you know it's working.

What starts as a conscious effort, over time, almost imperceptibly, begins to change you. Each time you step outside, even for just a moment, or bring a sliver of the natural world into your routine, you're allowing your life to find its natural rhythm again.

The cumulative power of these small, consistent doses of green cannot be overstated. They quietly rewire your senses, soothe your hurried thoughts, and gently remind you that you are part of something vast and ancient. Before you know it, forest bathing moves beyond an activity; it becomes a way of life. Your days become richer, your perspective widens, and the quiet magic of the natural world becomes a constant, comforting presence, part of your everyday.

CHAPTER NINETEEN

The Future of Forest Bathing

Sometimes, when I'm out in the quiet of the trees, I find myself wondering what forest bathing will look like in a hundred years. Will there be enough wild places left to truly practice it, to fully immerse ourselves? Because this powerful connection depends entirely on the existence of these green spaces. Right now, we're witnessing a swift decline: ancient woodlands vanishing for new roads and homes, green belts shrinking, trees lost in their thousands to disease, development, or simple neglect. It's difficult not to feel the growing chasm between what people deeply need for their well-being and what we, as a society, are actively choosing to protect.

Our growing understanding of nature's role isn't happening in a vacuum. It's built on the shoulders of incredible writers and pioneering scientists who have spent decades deepening our connection to the natural world. Think of the profound insights offered by authors like Robin Wall Kimmerer, whose work beautifully combines scientific understanding with Indigenous wisdom, or Peter Wohlleben, who blew me away when he revealed the secret lives of trees. Nature writers like Tristan Gooley, John Lewis-Stempel, and Simon Barnes have opened countless eyes to the wonders hidden in our landscapes. And underpinning so much of this is groundbreaking research by scientists like Suzanne Simard, who has shown us how trees communicate in vast, complex underground networks and how trees know which of their neighbours are direct offspring, pumping more nutrients to them than others! Their collective work strengthens the case for why we need to listen to nature more, because in reality we still know so little about our forests.

The Forest as a Lifeline

For many, forest bathing has become a lifeline. I've seen it help people reconnect with their senses, steady their breath, and find their footing again after grief, illness, or sheer exhaustion. But its effectiveness depends entirely on the forest itself. The rich soil, the unique scents, the intricate microbiome, the comforting birdsong, these aren't optional extras. They are the medicine. Lose that, and we forfeit something irreplaceable.

I look at the tiny oak saplings we've planted in our woodland and I wonder: will they still be alive in fifty years? How big will they be? How many species will they support? What turmoils will they witness? How many people will rest in their shade, or climb their branches and look out over the landscape? What will it look like? Will it be another housing estate covering the horizon?, or will the forest stretch itself out again and reclaim the land?

Every year, when I plant new trees, sow seeds or hide acorns in the leaf litter, these questions return to my mind, sometimes with a smile of hope, other days with a touch of fear or sadness.

Science Confirms What We've Always Felt

We know, without doubt, that spending time in nature helps us feel better. The science is increasingly clear, and what's exciting is understanding the full depth and range of these effects.

But there's a crucial element that often gets overlooked: the benefits are rooted in physical presence. You cannot download a forest, bottle its air, or replicate its full spectrum of therapeutic qualities with a headset.

Tech Can't Replace the Forest

Yes, we've explored apps and VR tools that aim to recreate forest experiences. They can offer a glimpse of nature to those isolated or far from green spaces. But they are not a substitute. At best, they're a pointer, a stepping stone back to the real thing.

The real risk comes when we start believing these digital versions are enough. When we convince ourselves we no longer need the unpredictability, the damp earth, or the textures of real trees. When a five-minute simulation slips into our screen-filled schedules and we start calling it "nature time."

I've tried those headsets. They're remarkably clever. But they can't replicate the invigorating cold on your cheeks, the surprise of a deer breaking cover, or the way low winter light glitters on morning frost. And they can't deliver the phytoncides, the beneficial soil microbes, or that deep, steadying sense of being connected to something far older than ourselves.

Forest Bathing as Stewardship

For me, forest bathing has evolved beyond pleasant walks or personal well-being. It's become a quiet act of stewardship. Once you've felt your body align with the land's rhythms, you inevitably develop a fierce desire to protect the places that offer such gifts.

I've seen countless local groups turn that care into action; replanting trees, restoring habitats, and patiently teaching children how to walk quietly and truly listen. My hope is to see this wave grow. Forest bathing doesn't have to be solitary or silent. It can be community-led, intergenerational, even a form of advocacy. It builds belonging, and with that comes shared responsibility.

There's potential, too, in responsible forest tourism, using immersive experiences to generate essential funds for land protection. But this must be handled with care, so we support rather than harm the very ecosystems we cherish.

A Personal Hope...

Honestly? My deepest hope is that the phrase "forest bathing" eventually becomes redundant.

I imagine a future where spending time in nature isn't seen as a prescribed activity, but simply a normal part of life. Where it's woven into school days, care homes, hospital treatment plans, and workplace policies. Where councils and governments treat green spaces not as decorative extras, but as essential infrastructure for human health.

I yearn for more rewilding projects, more city green corridors, and much wider access to real woods, not just the digital impression of them.

And personally? I hope we remember what it feels like to stand quietly in the trees, breathe out, and truly listen. Because once you've had that experience, once you've felt that deep connection, you'll fight harder than ever to protect it.

Chapter Twenty

Conclusion

You've made it to the end, or maybe it's the beginning. Because if you take nothing else from this book, I hope it's this: the forest is still waiting for you.

Not in some grand, remote wilderness you have to book months in advance and get a second mortgage to visit. Just... out there. Down the path behind your house. In the scrappy patch of green at the end of the lane. Along the hedgerows, in the city parks, under the old tree behind the bus stop.

There's a way back to yourself that doesn't involve fixing, improving, or achieving anything. Just show up. Stand still. Breathe. You don't have to be productive out there. You don't have to earn your rest. You're allowed to just *be*. Muddy, distracted, curious, tired. All of it.

And when you do? The forest won't judge. It doesn't care what you look like, what job you do, what's gone wrong this week. It just offers its ancient, living presence and says, *You're part of this too.*

But that's not all.

Because once you've felt that deep exhale in the trees, once you've noticed how your body reacts, how your thoughts slow, how your senses come back online, you realise it's a personal healing tool, and a free one at that. It's also a relationship. And with any relationship, there's a responsibility.

To protect what gives us life.
To speak up for places that can't speak for themselves.
To stop treating nature like a backdrop or a luxury, and start seeing it as kin.

We're not separate from the land. We *are* the land. What happens to the woods happens to us.

So let this book be a gentle push:

Put your phone on silent.

Go outside. Find a patch of green, however small.

Go slowly.

Let your senses lead.

Pay attention.

Say thank you.

Come back again.

Not because you're trying to master anything. But because this is where you remember what it means to belong.

If enough of us remember that, maybe we stand a chance of keeping these places wild. Maybe we become better guardians of the forests and the wider natural world.

And maybe, just maybe, we remember how to take better care of ourselves, too.

About the author

Joanne spent her early years growing up on a dairy farm in south-east England where her fascination with nature began. After a corporate career in software consultancy, which spanned 25 years, several continents, and numerous bouts of stress and exhaustion, Joanne quit the rat race in 2017 to follow her passions for wildlife and photography.

Enrolling on a one-year intensive training course, living in a tent in the African wilderness, Joanne re-trained as a professional safari guide, immersing herself in the flora and fauna of various sub-Saharan habitats through daily drives and bush walks.

Following graduation, she worked as a guide and later became the manager of a luxury bush camp in the Kafue National Park, Zambia, where she still freelances for a few months each year.

She appreciates that not everyone can disappear into the wilderness for 12 months to improve their physical and mental health, but she believes there are simple steps anyone can take to reconnect with nature and improve their general well-being.

Her favorite mantra is "The purpose of life is to live a life of purpose", and since the natural world has always inspired and helped her in such a profound way, she has become passionate about giving back, not only to nature but to others by sharing her knowledge, methods and tools through writing self-help books and educating her guests on safari.

She lives in the UK and when she's not writing, she spends her time rewilding a small piece of ancient woodland, making handmade nature-inspired jewelry and taking photographs. Find her on Instagram (@joannehedger) or scan this QR code with your camera to sign up for "Elemental Insights", delivered to your inbox 8 times a year.

Your Chance to Help Others...

Before we wrap up, I want to share why leaving a review on Amazon is so important. Not only does it help others find the guidance they're looking for, but your review also helps increase the book's visibility, allowing more people to discover the incredible benefits of forest bathing, people who might not have heard of it yet.

Now, we all know that reviews can sometimes be... shall we say.... a bit suspicious these days, thanks to AI-generated ones and fake ratings. Amazon is constantly working to clean that up, but there's a simple way you can make sure your review stays visible and authentic: include a photo!

Whether it's a snap of your paperback, your Kindle, or, if you're feeling adventurous, yourself reading the book out in nature, it helps add a personal touch that Amazon loves.

Thank you so much for your support, it means the world to me, and it's what helps this book reach the right people.

Blessings from among the trees,

Joanne x

Books by the Same Author

Revive and Thrive

Regenerative Gardening for a Sustainable Future

If you've ever looked out at your backyard and felt overwhelmed by weeds, lifeless soil, or the sheer effort of getting started, this book is for you.

You want a lush, thriving garden that feeds your family and the planet, but every guide you've read feels like a masterclass for experts, or worse, it's filled with methods that leave you feeling like you're doing more harm than good. You're not alone. And you're not stuck.

Right now, the world is at a tipping point. The United Nations says we're losing soil faster than we can replenish it, meaning future generations face a food crisis that begins beneath our feet. At the same time, prices at the supermarket keep climbing, while produce drenched in pesticides and full of micro-plastics, feels like the only option left.

The solution? Start where you are. Take control of your little patch of earth and transform it into a regenerative oasis. You don't need a sprawling farm or a fortune to make an impact, just the right tools, a clear plan, and a commitment to start.

Energetic Herbalism for Beginners

Radically Improve the Effectiveness of Healing Herbs by Matching The Energetic Power of Plants with People and Place.

Are you tired of relying on synthetic drugs that onlyseem to mask the problem, not solve it?

Have you wandered the aisles of health stores, filled with hope, only to try herbal remedies that didn't work for you, leaving you frustrated, out of pocket, and feeling like natural healing just isn't for you?

You're not alone. The truth is, the "one-size-fits-all" approach many products offer doesn't consider the unique needs of *your* body. That's where this book steps in.

Inside, you'll discover:

The 4 energetic constitutions and how to identify yours so you can start using herbs that truly resonate with your body.

The 6 tissue states a practical way to understand your body's signals and respond with the right remedies.

A no-nonsense guide to over 50 medicinal plants paired with their unique energetics, so you can finally match the right herb to your needs. No fluff. No guesswork. Just straightforward, actionable knowledge that empowers you to make herbalism work for *you*.

This book is for anyone who's ready to take back control of their health, without the side effects, without the disappointment, and without feeling overwhelmed.

Dream Interpretation for Better Sleep

Find Meaning in the Messages of Your Subconscious Mind to Build Your Own Dream Dictionary

Ever wake up from a dream and wonder why the symbols feel so vivid, yet so puzzling? The truth is, interpreting dreams isn't as simple as looking up a symbol in a dictionary. A "this-for-that" approach, like "cats mean independence" or "water means emotions", is too generic to be useful. Why? Because you are not everyone else. The meaning of a symbol can change depending on who you are and how you view the world. For example, a cat could represent warmth and affection to a cat lover, or it could trigger irritation for someone with allergies. And that same cat could be a playful kitten in your dream, or a fierce lion, which would send a very different message.

This book doesn't rely on those one-size-fits-all interpretations. Instead, it helps you decode the unique language of your own dreams, one that's personal to you and your experiences.

References

- **Forest or Nature Bathing: Ancient Practices, Modern Uses**
  https://www.bluezones.com/2019/06/forest-or-nature-bathing-ancient-practices-modern-uses-and-the-science-of-relaxation

- **Effect of forest bathing trips on human immune function**
  https://www.ncbi.nlm.nih.gov/pmc/articles/PMC2793341

- **The physiological effects of Shinrin-yoku (taking in the forest atmosphere)**
  https://www.ncbi.nlm.nih.gov/pmc/articles/PMC2793346

- **Biophilia hypothesis | Description, Nature, & Human Behavior**
  https://www.britannica.com/science/biophilia-hypothesis

- **Urban Forest Bathing: How to Find Pockets of Nature in the City**
  https://vacayou.com/magazine/urban-forest-bathing

- **Day Hiking Essentials Checklist**
  https://www.rei.com/learn/expert-advice/day-hiking-checklist.html

- **How to Practice Mindfulness in Nature**
  https://mindfulnessexercises.com/how-to-practice-mindfulness-in-nature

- **The 7 Principles – Leave No Trace Center for Outdoor Ethics**
  https://lnt.org/why/7-principles

- **The little-known physical and mental health benefits of urban trees**
  https://yaleclimateconnections.org/2023/02/the-little-known-physical-and-mental-health-benefits-of-urban-trees

- **Mindful Garden Design – How To Create A Mindfulness Outdoor Space**
  https://garden-care.org.uk/health-wellbeing/mindful-garden-design-how-to-create-a-mindfulness-outdoor-space

- **COMMUNITY ENGAGEMENT RESOURCE GUIDE**
  https://www.nrpa.org/contentassets/19b3cbe05a634d5e8d3b712dbc8aa9d0/community-engagement-guide-nrpa.pdf

- **Gardening for health: a regular dose of gardening**
  https://www.ncbi.nlm.nih.gov/pmc/articles/PMC6334070

- **The science of forest bathing: 5 ways it can boost health**
  https://www.npr.org/2023/08/22/1195337204/a-guide-to-forest-bathing

- **Seasonal Forest Changes of Color and Temperature**

https://www.ncbi.nlm.nih.gov/pmc/articles/PMC10378933

- **Ethical Foraging 101: What You Need to Know**
  https://learningherbs.com/skills/foraging

- **Your guide to forest bathing – Forestry England**
  https://www.forestryengland.uk/blog/forest-bathing

- **Why Being (Alone) in Nature Is Good for You**
  https://www.psychologytoday.com/us/blog/solitude-in-social-world/202203/why-being-alone-in-nature-is-good-you

- **Is it safe to stay in the forest at night?**
  https://www.quora.com/Is-it-safe-to-stay-in-the-forest-at-night

- **How nature can help with Seasonal Affective Disorder**
  https://www.theweathernetwork.com/en/news/lifestyle/health/how-nature-can-help-with-seasonal-affective-disorder

- **Nature-Based Mindfulness: A Qualitative Study**
  https://www.ncbi.nlm.nih.gov/pmc/articles/PMC10048623

- **How nature benefits mental health – Mind UK**
  https://www.mind.org.uk/information-support/tips-for-everyday-living/nature-and-mental-health/how-nature-benefits-mental-health

- **8 National Parks With Exceptional Accessibility for Visitors With Disabilities**
  https://www.ecowatch.com/national-parks-disability-accessibility.html

- **"Give me a break!" A systematic review and meta-analysis**

on green space breaks
https://www.ncbi.nlm.nih.gov/pmc/articles/PMC9432722

- **Forest Bathing International**
https://www.forestbathinginternational.org

- **Indigenous people and nature: a tradition of conservation**
https://www.unep.org/news-and-stories/story/indigenous-people-and-nature-tradition-conservation

- **International Forest Therapy Days**
https://www.foresttherapydays.com

- **Forest Bathing Benefits: Why Winter Is the Best Time of Year**
https://www.thezoereport.com/wellness/forest-bathing-benefits

- **Can you make a living as a forest therapy guide?**
https://www.forestbathing.club/journal/2021/3/2/can-you-make-a-living-as-a-forest-therapy-guide

- **Community Gardens: Lessons Learned From California**
https://www.ncbi.nlm.nih.gov/pmc/articles/PMC1447988

- **Benefits of Environmental Volunteering – Earth5R**
https://earth5r.org/benefits-of-environmental-volunteering-with-earth5r

- **Creating Accessible and Inclusive Meetings or Events – Rutgers ODS**
https://ods.rutgers.edu/resources/creating-accessible-events

- **Why Biophilic Design Is Crucial in the Workplace and**

Beyond
https://www.gensler.com/blog/why-biophilic-design-is-crucial-in-workplace

- **The Transformative Power of Journaling Outdoors for Your Mental Health**
https://ccbhc.org/journaling-for-mental-health

- **Digital Detox: Why We Need It – Newport Academy**
https://www.newportacademy.com/resources/restoring-families/digital-detox

- **The calming and cognitive-enhancing effects of nature exposure**:
Bratman, G. N., Hamilton, J. P., & Daily, G. C. (2012). *The impacts of nature experience on human cognitive function and mental health. Annals of the New York Academy of Sciences, 1249*(1), 118–136.
https://doi.org/10.1111/j.1749-6632.2011.06400.x

- **A framework for understanding how nature affects well-being**:
Kuo, M. (2015). *How might contact with nature promote human health? Promising mechanisms and a possible central pathway. Frontiers in Psychology, 6*, 1093.
https://doi.org/10.3389/fpsyg.2015.01093

- **Establishing a research agenda on nature and health connections**:
Frumkin, H., Bratman, G. N., Breslow, S. J., Cochran, B., Kahn, P. H. Jr., Lawler, J. J., ... & Wood, S. A. (2017). *Nature contact and human health: A research agenda. Environmental Health Perspectives, 125*(7), 075001.

https://doi.org/10.1289/EHP1663

- **Global evidence supporting green spaces as public health essentials**:
World Health Organization. (2016). *Urban green spaces and health: A review of evidence*. WHO Regional Office for Europe. https://www.euro.who.int/en/publications/abstracts/urban-green-spaces-and-health-a-review-of-evidence-2016

Printed in Dunstable, United Kingdom